BITS ON STICKS

BITS ON STICKS

JOHN MCLEAY

NEW HOLLAND

CONTENTS

INTRODUCTION   7

MEATY STICKS   8

FISHY STICKS   52

BIRDY STICKS   84

VEGGIE STICKS   118

RETRO STICKS   140

SWEET STICKS   160

SAUCES   174

GLOSSARY   186

INDEX   188

ACKNOWLEDGEMENTS   191

INTRODUCTION

For as long as I remember I've always loved barbecues. As a kid, I have many a fond memory of hot summer nights, some games in the backyard and the enticing aroma wafting from the direction of the barbecue.

Nowadays, whether it's with a group of friends, or just the wife, there is still something special about throwing a variety of different things on the barbecue, making a few of salads, enjoying some drinks and great company. Being a chef there is a certain expectation placed on you when entertaining—sausages and fatty chops are just not going to cut it when it comes to satisfying my guests. I guess this is how I first became interested in cooking with skewers.

Being always short of time, I discovered that it was so easy to buy a few varieties of meats, cut them up and throw them in a couple of different marinades overnight. The next day, it was as easy as threading them onto some skewers and wham, bam my friends were impressed.

There are varying theories on when and how skewers where invented, one of the more popular being that the soldiers of Turkic tribes would skewer meat on their swords and cook them over open field fires as they pushed west from their homelands in Central Asia. One thing is certain, since then skewering food has certainly been embraced the world over. It seems as though every culture has its own version of meat on a stick. In Asia, alone, there are countless varying versions of satay that not only vary from country to country but also from region to region. Even the skewers themselves vary dramatically, not only in appearance but also in size. From the common simple bamboo variety used extensively throughout Asia to the ornate mini sword-like variety found throughout the Middle East.

Putting together the recipes for this book has been an enjoyable task for me as it gave me a chance to revisit some old recipes as well as create some new. And being a chef that cooks southeast Asian food it was interesting to work with other styles of food, although I'm sure my love of Asian food probably shines through.

Before I leave you to your cooking I would like to leave you with a few little tips. Firstly it's a bit of a necessity if using bamboo skewers to soak them in water for at least a few hours before using them—this will stop them burning. And if using a chargrill, try and use metal skewers as the grill flames could turn your bamboo skewer into a charcoal one.

Try and buy a few of the ornate Middle Eastern-style skewers as the look fantastic and they go so well with so many of the recipes. You'll be able to source them from Middle Eastern grocery stores.

And finally don't think you need to follow the recipes exactly. If you're not a great lover of garlic simply reduce the amount you put in—the same goes for chilli.

I hope you enjoy the book. Happy skewering.

John McLeay

MEATY STICKS

ARGENTINEAN BEEF WITH CHIMICHURRI

Argentina is known the world over for its beef, so in my opinion there is no way they could get a beef recipe wrong. These simple skewers are a testament to my theory.

750g (1lb 10oz) aged beef fillet, cleaned
    and cut into 3cm (1½in) cubes
vegetable oil, for the grill
4 long metal skewers

CHIMICHURRI
4 cups flat-leaf parsley leaves
7 garlic cloves

½ teaspoon freshly ground black pepper
½ teaspoon smoked paprika
4 tablespoons fresh oregano leaves, chopped
3 tablespoons lemon juice
4 tablespoons red wine vinegar
1 teaspoon sea salt
½ teaspoon chilli flakes
150ml (5fl oz) olive oil

In a blender, place all of the chimichurri ingredients and blend into a rough paste.

Put the beef in a bowl, spoon in 4 tablespoons of the chimichurri, and mix together. Cover and allow the beef to marinate in the refrigerator for 30 minutes.

Thread the beef evenly onto the skewers. Cook the skewers over high heat on the chargrill, turning occasionally, for around 3 to 4 minutes.

Remove the skewers from the grill and place them on a serving platter, spoon over the remaining chimichurri and serve with lemon.

Serves 4

> TIP
> OK, it may be a little unconventional,
> but I adore eating these delicious
> skewers with a fennel, rocket,
> red radish and red onion salad.

BARBECUE PORK AND LYCHEE STICKS

A combo of two things I adore. I can't resist the barbecue pork hanging up in Chinese chopshop windows—it's just so decadently delicious. And fresh lychees are one of my favourite fruits.

850g (1lb 12oz) pork fillet, fat and sinew removed,
    cut into 2½cm (1in) pieces
vegetable oil, for the grill or pan
15 lychees, skinned, halved and pips removed
10 skewers

MARINADE
1½ tablespoons honey

2 tablespoons hoisin sauce
1½ tablespoons light soy sauce
2 tablespoons shaoxing (Chinese rice) wine
1 teaspoon five spice powder
1 tablespoon sesame oil
½ teaspoon ginger powder
¼ teaspoon ground white pepper
3 drops red food colouring

Put all the marinade ingredients into a bowl, and mix together well. Add the pork and continue to mix, making sure the pork is fully coated with the marinade. Cover and put in the refrigerator to marinate overnight.

When ready to cook, remove the pork from the marinade and use absorbent paper to pat off excess liquid. Thread four pieces of pork, alternating with three lychee halves, onto each stick.

Preheat a flat grill or frying pan, add a little oil and cook the sticks on medium to high heat for around 5 minutes.

Makes 10

BO LA LOT (BEEF WRAPPED IN BETEL LEAF)

BO LA LOT
(BEEF WRAPPED IN BETEL LEAF)

These tasty little morsels remind me vividly of an old lady, on her haunches, cooking these skewers on a wire rack over open coals, on a street in Saigon. Simply slide the little parcels off the skewers, dunk them in nuoc cham and enjoy an authentic taste from Saigon.

400g (14oz) beef mince (ground beef) (a little fatty is best)
4 tablespoons roasted unsalted peanuts, chopped
5cm (2in) piece lemongrass, white part only, chopped finely
1 teaspoon caster (superfine) sugar
2 tablespoons fish sauce
2 teaspoon five spice powder

1 spring onion (scallions), chopped
2 teaspoons sesame oil
1 garlic clove, peeled and finely chopped
30 large betel leaves
vegetable oil, for the grill or pan
nuoc cham (see Sauces)
6 skewers

Combine all the ingredients, except the betel leaves and the nuoc cham, in a bowl and mix well.

Divide the mixture among the betel leaves, taking care not to overfill them. Fold down the sides of each leaf then roll it into a neat parcel, making sure the mixture is fully enclosed by each leaf.

Thread five parcels onto either a thin metal skewer or a wooden skewer, and repeat until you have six skewers. Brush with a little oil and grill or barbecue for about 2 minutes each side.

Serve the skewers with nuoc cham.

Makes 30

TIP
Betel leaves are a hardy dark green leaf. They are an integral part of the recipe as no other leaf is suitable. You can generally get them at good Asian markets or try a fruit and vegetable store.

BURMESE PORK SKEWERS

A lot of Burmese food seems to have Indian origins, I've tried to figure this out but keep drawing blanks (Wikipedia and Google weren't very helpful). My only explanation is that Indians live throughout Southeast Asia and I'm sensing that, as in Malaysia, they have left their culinary footprint in Burma (Myanmar). This recipe popped up in a Burmese cookbook I bought a few years ago. I'm pretty sure the recipe would have evolved since then, so I'm comfortable sharing it.

500g (17½oz) pork fillet, cleaned and cut into
   bite-sized pieces
vegetable oil, for the grill or pan
8 skewers

MARINADE
2 garlic cloves, chopped
2 lemongrass stalks, white part only, chopped finely
2 large red chillies, chopped
1 small handful coriander (cilantro), chopped
2 small shallots (eschalots), peeled and chopped
1cm (½in) piece ginger, peeled and finely grated
2 teaspoons garam masala
½ teaspoon turmeric powder
1 teaspoon caster (superfine) sugar
1 tablespoon fish sauce
2 tablespoons rice wine

Put the pork pieces into a bowl.

Put the garlic, lemongrass, chillies, coriander, shallots and ginger in a mortar and pestle and pound to a rough paste. Alternatively, you can mix them in a food processor. Add the garam masala, turmeric powder, caster sugar, fish sauce and the rice wine. Pour this mixture over the pork, mix through, cover and refrigerate for at least 1 hour.

Thread four pieces of the marinated pork onto a skewer, and repeat the process until all the pork is used up.

If you're cooking on a barbecue, place the skewers onto the hot chargrill and cook for around 5 minutes, turning occasionally. Otherwise, pour a little oil into a frying pan and cook for around the same time.

Makes 8

HAITIAN VOODOO STICKS (SPICY BEEF KEBABS)

I'm not sure where I came across these deliciously spicy numbers. All I remember is seeing their name and thinking, 'Whoa! I gotta try them!' A word of warning though: they have a serious kick to them.

700g (1lb 9oz) beef sirloin or rump, cleaned and
    cut into 2cm (1in) cubes
vegetable oil, for the grill or pan
2 onions, peeled and cut into 2cm (1in) cubes
8–10 skewers

MARINADE
2 teaspoons cayenne pepper
1 teaspoon ground black pepper
2 teaspoons ground cumin
½ teaspoon salt
4 garlic cloves, peeled and minced
50ml (1¾fl oz) vegetable oil

In a bowl, mix together the cayenne, black pepper, cumin, salt, garlic and oil. Add the beef, mix well, cover and marinate for 2 hours.

Thread the beef and the onion onto the skewers. Add a little oil to a pan or grill and cook the skewers over medium heat, turning occasionally, for around 4 minutes. The beef should still be a little pink in the middle.

Makes 8 to 10, depending on your threading skills

ISSAN SAUSAGES

Issan is an area in northeast Thailand that is famous for its food, and I can see absolutely why. I love these delicious sausages. You'll find them everywhere in stalls on the streets of Thailand—I think they are the perfect late-night snack. They're sold in two varieties—freshly made or fermented. I prefer the fermented, but since it's a bit tricky to get the fermentation process right, we'll stick to the fresh.

50g (1¾oz) or about 1 metre (3 feet) sausage casing
500g (17½oz) fatty pork mince (ground pork)
10 coriander (cilantro) seeds, roasted and ground
1 cup cooked jasmine rice
5 garlic cloves, peeled and chopped
1 tablespoon caster (superfine) sugar

2 tablespoons fish sauce
1½ tablespoons rice vinegar
1 lemongrass stalk, white part only, chopped finely
vegetable oil, for the grill or pan
sweet chilli sauce (see Sauces)
8 skewers

Wash the sausage casing in water and a little vinegar. Set aside for later use.

In a large bowl, place the pork, ground coriander, cooked rice, garlic, caster sugar, fish sauce, rice vinegar and lemongrass and mix together well.

Fit a wide nozzle to a piping bag then feed the sausage casing onto the piping nozzle. When you get to the end of the sausage casing, tie a knot in it. Fill the piping bag up with the sausage mixture and pipe the mixture into the casing, twisting the casing as you go to make small round sausages (this can be a bit tricky at first). If you're having trouble linking the sausages, simply tie them with a piece of string as you're going. When you get to the end of the casing, tie it off. You should now have a long chain of sausages.

If you have time, allow the sausages to rest in the refrigerator for 24 hours, preferably hanging. You can use them straight away, but they won't be as tasty or stable though.

When you are ready to cook, cut them into lengths of three sausages and feed them onto skewers. Cook in a lightly oiled frying pan or the flat grill on a barbecue for around 5 minutes.

Serve with lettuce cups and sweet chilli sauce, coriander, crispy shallots and chopped peanuts.

Serves 4

> TIP
> Ask your butcher to organise some
> sausage casing for you.

LEMON AND OREGANO LAMB SKEWERS

These are a quintessential Greek lamb skewer. They are perfect served with tzatziki, some pita bread and a Greek salad.

600g (1lb 5oz) lamb strap, cleaned of all sinew
vegetable oil, for the grill or pan
4 skewers
tzatziki (see Sauces)

MARINADE
3 tablespoons oregano leaves, chopped
1 garlic clove, peeled and finely chopped
1 large pinch ground white pepper
1 large pinch table salt
½ teaspoon grated lemon rind
1 lemon, juiced
3 tablespoons olive oil

Cut the lamb into roughly 3cm (1½in) cubes and place in a bowl. Add all the marinade ingredients and mix well. Cover and refrigerate for at least 4 hours.

Thread the lamb onto the skewers. Place the skewers on a lightly oiled barbecue or in a frying pan and cook on high heat, turning occasionally, for around 5 minutes. Remove from the heat and rest for 4 minutes before eating.

Serve with pita bread, some tzatziki and a Greek salad.

Serves 4

LEMONGRASS AND SESAME BEEF SKEWERS

LEMONGRASS AND SESAME BEEF SKEWERS

These Vietnamese-inspired skewers are so simple and really easy to make. They're equally good by themselves, or served with rice paper and a salad with heaps of fresh herbs, such as Vietnamese mint, mint, coriander (cilantro), Thai basil and shiso.

600g (1lb 5oz) good quality beef—I like to use
    eye fillet or porterhouse
vegetable oil, for the grill or pan
1 tablespoon sesame seeds, toasted (garnish)
1 handful coriander (cilantro) leaves (garnish)
8 skewers

MARINADE
2 shallots (eschalots), finely chopped
1 garlic clove, finely chopped
2 lemongrass stalks, white part only, finely chopped
2 large red chillies, seeded and chopped
3 tablespoons coriander (cilantro), chopped
2 tablespoons fish sauce
1 tablespoon sesame oil
1 tablespoon vegetable oil
1 tablespoon caster (superfine) sugar
1 tablespoon lime juice
2 tablespoons sesame seeds, toasted

Combine the shallots, garlic, lemongrass, chillies and coriander in a mortar and pestle (you could also use a bar or stick blender) and grind to form a rough paste. Place the paste into a mixing bowl and add the fish sauce, oils, sugar, lime juice and the sesame seeds, and stir well to combine.

Cut the meat into reasonably thin square shapes. Place the meat in the bowl with the marinade, and give it a stir to make sure all the meat is coated. Cover and allow to sit in the refrigerator for at least 5 hours.

Thread three pieces of beef onto each skewer. Cook on a lightly oiled flat grill or frying pan on high heat for around 1 minute each side.

Remove from the heat and allow to rest for a few minutes before serving.

Garnish with a sprinkle of toasted sesame and coriander leaves.

Makes 8

MINCED PORK ON LEMONGRASS STICKS

As these skewers cook, the lemongrass imparts a beautiful flavour to the pork. Once cooked, remove the lemongrass and place the pork in a crusty baguette with cucumber, chilli, herbs and a scrambled egg.

10 lemongrass stalks, outer leaves removed
600g (1lb 5oz) pork mince (ground pork)
2 garlic cloves, peeled and minced
4 shallots (eschalots), peeled and chopped
1 teaspoon sugar
2 tablespoons rice flour

1½ tablespoons fish sauce
½ teaspoon freshly ground black pepper
2 drops red food colouring
vegetable oil, for the grill or pan
nuoc cham (see Sauces)

Cut the base and the top off the lemongrass then cut the lemongrass into 15cm (6in) lengths, and set aside for later use.

In a bowl combine the pork, garlic, shallots, sugar, rice flour, fish sauce, black pepper and food colouring. Mix well. Divide the mixture into 12 portions and roll each portion into a sausage shape. Insert the lemongrass skewer into each portion and refrigerate for at least 1 hour.

Heat the flat grill of a barbecue and cook the skewers, turning regularly, for about 5 minutes.
Makes 10

NONYA PORK SATAY WITH PINEAPPLE SATAY SAUCE

Nonya cuisine came about as the result of Chinese migration to Malaysia and Singapore. It's known for its use of fragrant ingredients, such as galangal, lemongrass and turmeric, as well as the use of tamarind, belacan (shrimp paste) and candlenuts.

500g (17½oz) pork neck or fillet, cut into
    3cm (1½in) pieces
vegetable oil, for the grill or pan
10 skewers

SPICE PASTE
1cm (½in) piece belacan (shrimp paste)
3 tablespoons tamarind pulp
8 macadamia or Brazil nuts

2 lemongrass stalks white part only, finely chopped
2 garlic cloves, peeled and crushed
1 teaspoon ground cumin
1 teaspoon ground coriander (cilantro)
4 shallots (eschalots), peeled, finely chopped
1 tablespoon brown sugar
2 bird's eye chillies, chopped
100ml (3½fl oz) coconut milk
50ml (1¾fl oz) vegetable oil

Place the belacan in foil and roast it in a hot oven for 10 minutes. For the spice paste, place all the ingredients, including the shrimp paste, in a blender and blend to a semi-smooth paste.

    Place the pork and the spice paste in a mixing bowl, cover and refrigerate overnight or at least 2 hours.

    Thread three or four pieces of pork onto each skewer. Brush each skewer with a little oil and chargrill or cook on a flat grill turning occasionally for around 8 minutes.

    Serve with pineapple satay sauce (recipe on following page).

Makes 10

PINEAPPLE SATAY SAUCE

3 shallots (eschalots), peeled and sliced
2 garlic cloves, peeled and finely chopped
1 lemongrass stalk, white part only, finely chopped
1 teaspoon turmeric powder
5cm (2in) piece ginger, finely grated
3 large red chillies, seeded and chopped
1 teaspoon belacan (shrimp paste)

50ml (1¾fl oz) vegetable oil
150ml (5fl oz) coconut milk
100g (3½oz) pineapple, blended to a pulp
150g (5oz) roasted peanuts, crushed
4 tablespoons tamarind pulp
½ teaspoon salt
1 tablespoon brown sugar

Place the shallots, garlic, lemongrass, turmeric powder, ginger, chillies and belacan in a blender, and blend to a smooth paste.

Heat the oil in a saucepan, and fry the blender contents for around 2 minutes. Add the coconut milk, pineapple pulp, peanuts, tamarind, salt and sugar.

Bring to the boil while stirring, turn down to a simmer and cook for 15 minutes stirring occasionally. Pour into a clean container and allow to cool.

Makes around 600ml (21fl oz)

NONYA PORK SATAY WITH PINEAPPLE SATAY SAUCE

PEPPERED VENISON, BEETROOT AND CARAMELISED SHALLOT PINTXOS

Venison is an extremely lean meat and because of that it becomes very dry if you overcook it, so it's extremely important that you keep your skewers medium rare or under. Pintxos are basically small skewers—a very popular Spanish tapas. If it's available. use kangaroo instead of venison.

10 small baby beetroots
10 shallots (eschalots)
100ml (3½fl oz) red wine
1 tablespoon caster (superfine) sugar
300g (10¼oz) venison fillets, cut into bite-sized
    pieces

50ml (1¾fl oz) vegetable oil
1 teaspoon cracked black pepper
¼ teaspoon salt
vegetable oil for the grill or pan
10 small skewers

In a saucepan, cover the beetroots with water, bring to the boil and then reduce to a simmer until the beets are cooked through. Strain the water, then slip off the skins.

In a saucepan, cover the shallots with water, bring to the boil and then simmer for 5 minutes. Strain, then place the shallots in iced water. Remove the skins and cut off the root ends.

Place the red wine and sugar in a saucepan and bring to the boil, then reduce to a simmer. Add the shallots and cook while swirling for 7 minutes.

Put the venison in a mixing bowl with the oil, pepper and salt, and mix together.

Thread a piece of venison meat, a shallot and a beetroot onto each skewer. Cook on a lightly oiled preheated flat grill or frying pan for 1 minute each side. The meat should be rare. Allow to rest for a few minutes before eating.

Serve with salsa verde.

Makes 10

PINCHOS MORUNOS (SPANISH-STYLE SKEWERS)

A popular item in tapas bars, these skewers come from the Andalusia area. They are generally made with either chicken or pork. Although there are countless versions of the marinade, paprika, garlic, cumin and coriander (cilantro) are the essential ingredients.

500g (17½oz) pork fillet cut into 1½cm (¾in) cubes
15 small skewers

MARINADE
2 garlic cloves, peeled and finely chopped
1 teaspoon ground cumin
4 tablespoons olive oil

1 teaspoon smoked paprika
1 teaspoon coriander (cilantro) powder
1 pink saffron threads
1 tablespoon red wine vinegar
1 small handful of flat-leaf parsley leaves, chopped
¼ teaspoon salt

In a blender, blend together all of the marinade ingredients. Pour the marinade into a bowl, add the pork and mix through. Cover and refrigerate overnight or for at least 2 hours.

Thread three pieces of meat onto each skewer and cook on a hot barbecue for around 3 to 4 minutes. Serve with lemon.

Makes 15

POMEGRANATE GOAT SKEWERS

I consider goat to be an un-appreciated meat. It has terrific flavour and is quite versatile. The Moroccan flavours in this dish go brilliantly with the goat and the tartness of the pomegranate.

800g (1lb 12oz) boneless goat leg meat, all sinew
    removed
vegetable oil for the grill or pan
50ml (1¾fl oz) pomegranate molasses, extra
    (to serve)
8 skewers

MARINADE
50ml (1¾fl oz) pomegranate molasses
1 tablespoon ground cumin
1 tablespoon smoked paprika
½ teaspoon cayenne pepper
½ teaspoon sea salt
¼ teaspoon ground cloves
1 teaspoon allspice powder
½ teaspoon ground turmeric
50ml (1¾fl oz) olive oil

In a bowl, mix together all of the marinade ingredients. Cut the goat into 2cm (1in) cubes, add to the marinade and mix through. Cover and refrigerate for at least 2 hours.

Thread four or five pieces onto each skewer and cook on a preheated barbecue or in a frying pan on medium–high heat for around 6 minutes. Remove the skewers, and drizzle over a little of the pomegranate molasses.

Serve with couscous or a chickpea (garbanzo bean), parsley and pomegranate salad.

Serves 4

PORK BELLY WITH CHILLI CARAMEL

PORK BELLY WITH CHILLI CARAMEL

Red Spice Road and pork belly go hand in hand. There is not a chance in hell I could ever take it off the menu. To say it's popular is a bit of an understatement—it's all our customers ever seem to talk about. This being the case, I thought I had better give you a slightly simpler stick version. I like to serve this version of the belly in large shot glasses. You'll need 15 shot glasses for this recipe.

700g (1lb 8 oz) piece pork belly
200ml (7fl oz) light soy sauce
2 cups water
3 tablespoons caster (superfine) sugar
6 star anise
15 small skewers

CHILLI CARAMEL
500g (17½oz) caster (superfine) sugar
500ml (17fl oz) water
2 small red chillies, chopped
12 star anise
200ml (7fl oz) fish sauce
100ml (3½fl oz) water, extra

TO SERVE
100ml (3fl oz) light soy sauce
2 cups tapioca starch
5 tablespoons five spice powder
1 litre (36fl oz) vegetable oil
75ml (2½fl oz) black vinegar

GARNISH
2 large red chillies, seeded and sliced
1 spring onion (scallions), finely sliced
4 tablespoons crispy fried shallots
1 small Granny Smith apple, peeled, and
    cut into small dice

Place the belly in a baking tray. In a bowl mix together the soy sauce, water, sugar and star anise then pour it in to the baking tray. Cover with non-stick baking paper (parchment paper) and foil and place in an oven preheated to 180°C (350°F). Cook for around 4 hours, checking occasionally to make sure the liquid has not reduced too much—if it has, top up with a little more water. Allow to cool slightly, then remove the belly. Place it on a tray, and refrigerate. When chilled completely, cut the pork belly into 2cm (1in) cubes.

Meanwhile, prepare the chilli caramel. In a saucepan, add the sugar and water and bring to the boil. Continue to boil until the mixture starts to caramelise. Add the chillies, star anise and fish sauce, being careful that the caramel does not splash you, as it becomes extremely hot. Turn down the heat and simmer for 5 minutes. Add the extra water, turn off completely and leave for 5 minutes.

Strain and set aside for later use.
Put the cold pork pieces into a bowl, add the soy sauce, mix to coat the belly and then pour off the soy sauce. Add the tapioca starch and the five spice powder and gently mix, making sure you coat the pork pieces evenly. Dust off any excess starch and set the pork aside ready for cooking.

Heat the oil in a wok or large saucepan to roughly 170°C (335°F)—test the temperature by dropping a piece of pork in the oil: it should sizzle as soon as it hits the oil. Add the coated pork pieces to the wok, being careful that the oil doesn't boil over. You may need to cook the pork in a few batches to keep the oil temperature at the right level. Fry each batch of pork for around 5 minutes, then remove from the oil and place on absorbent paper.

Place the cooked pork in a bowl, add the black vinegar and carefully toss the belly pieces so that they are coated in the vinegar. Drain the vinegar off, pour in a little chilli caramel and move the pork around so it gets coated in the caramel.

Thread two pieces of pork belly onto the end of each skewer, and repeat until you have prepared 15 skewers.

Pour some chilli caramel into the shot glasses, place a pork skewer in each glass, then scatter the chillies, spring onion, fried shallots and apple over the skewers.

Makes 15

TIP

Be extremely careful when deep-frying at home: always make sure the pot is bigger than you think you'll need to ensure there are no boil-overs.

SATE BABI MANIS

What sets these Indonesian sate sticks apart from the crowd is that they are pretty heavy on the sweet soy sauce (ketjap manis). They are served with a fairly simple soy and peanut dipping sauce

800g (1lb 12oz) pork neck, diced into 2cm (¾in) pieces
50ml (1¾fl oz) vegetable oil
10–12 skewers

MARINADE
2cm (1in) piece galangal, peeled and finely grated
1 teaspoon cumin seeds, roasted
2 shallots (eschalots), peeled and finely sliced
2 teaspoons coriander (cilantro) seeds, roasted
100ml (3½fl oz) dark sweet soy sauce (ketjap manis)

50ml (1¾fl oz) soy sauce
3 tablespoons lime juice
¼ teaspoon ground black pepper

DIPPING SAUCE
2 shallots (eschalots), peeled and finely diced
150ml (5fl oz) sweet soy sauce (ketjap manis)
50ml (1¾fl oz) light soy sauce
2 bird's eye chillies, deseeded and chopped
3 tablespoons peanuts, chopped

In a mortar and pestle, pound the galangal, cumin, shallots and coriander. Transfer the pounded spices to a bowl, and add both soy sauces, lime juice and the pepper. Add the pork to the bowl and mix well. Cover and leave to marinate in the refrigerator for at least 2 hours.

Meanwhile, make the dipping sauce. In a bowl, mix the sauce ingredients together.

Thread three or four pieces of pork onto each skewer. Brush the oil over the skewers and cook on a chargrill or flat grill. When cooked, remove from the heat.

Serve with the dipping sauce.

Makes 10 to 12

SUMAC AND ZATAR LAMB SKEWERS

I live in the middle of a Middle-Eastern and Turkish hub. I love strolling up the street and exploring the grocery stores and checking out the diverse range of herbs and spices on offer. Sumac would have to be one of my favourites—I love its lemon-like zing and its fantastic purple-red colour.

700g (1lb 9oz) lamb loin, cleaned and cut into
   2½cm (1in) cubes
vegetable oil, for the grill or pan
4 long skewers

MARINADE
2 garlic cloves, peeled and chopped
4 shallots (eschalots), peeled and chopped
1 tablespoon sumac

1 tablespoon zatar
1 teaspoon ground allspice powder
1 teaspoon finely grated lemon rind
2 tablespoons lemon juice
1 teaspoon salt
1 small handful flat-leaf parsley leaves,
   roughly chopped
50ml (1¾fl oz) vegetable oil

In a blender or a food processor, combine all the marinade ingredients and blend into a smooth paste. Spoon the marinade into a bowl, and add the lamb. Mix well. Cover and leave to marinate overnight.

Remove the lamb from the marinade and thread it onto four long skewers. Cook the skewers over high heat, turning occasionally, for about 5 minutes.

Serve with warm pita bread, tabouleh and some yoghurt.

Serves 4

WAGYU AND RICE MEATBALLS WITH A QUICK RED CURRY

Wagyu beef has a higher fat content than your everyday beef, which is a good thing when it comes to meatballs, as they stay moist. This recipe makes a fair number of meatballs, so any you don't use can be put in the freezer for later use. This dish also looks great served in tall shot glasses.

1kg (2lb 4oz) wagyu beef mince (ground wagyu beef)
1 handful coriander (cilantro) leaves, chopped
1 spring onion (scallions), chopped
75ml (2½fl oz) fish sauce
2 large red chillies, chopped
1 lemongrass stalk, white part only, finely chopped
3 teaspoons caster (superfine) sugar
2 garlic cloves, peeled and finely chopped
250g (9oz) cooked jasmine rice
vegetable oil, for the baking tray
35 fork toothpicks

RED CURRY
50ml (1¾fl oz) vegetable oil
4 soaked dried chillies, chopped
½ red onion, peeled and sliced
1 lemongrass stalk, white part only, finely chopped
1 garlic clove, peeled and chopped
3 kaffir lime leaves, finely chopped
2cm (1in) piece ginger, peeled and finely chopped
50g (1¾oz) palm sugar or brown sugar
50ml (1¾fl oz) fish sauce
600ml (21fl oz) coconut milk

GARNISH
fried crispy shallots
coriander, chopped

To make the curry, heat the oil in a wok or saucepan and add the chillies, onion, lemongrass, garlic, kaffir lime and ginger. Cook while stirring for around 5 minutes. Add the palm sugar and the fish sauce and continue to cook until the palm sugar has dissolved.

Transfer the mixture to a blender and blend to a smooth paste. Put the paste in a saucepan, add the coconut milk and bring to a simmer. Cook for 5 minutes.

Meanwhile, prepare the meatballs. In a bowl, mix together all the ingredients thoroughly. Roll the meatballs into 35g (1¼oz) balls and place them on a lightly oiled baking tray. Cook them in a preheated oven on high (220°C or 420°F) for around 10 minutes.

To serve, put a fork toothpick into each meatball. Pour a little curry into small glasses and top with a meatball. If you like, garnish with some crispy shallots and chopped coriander.

Makes 35

XINJIANG LAMB KEBAB

Xinjiang is an area in northwestern China, inhabited by the Uighur people, who are largely practising Muslims. Lamb is their meat of choice. Depending on your taste, you can use lamb loin or back strap if you like your meat lean, or lamb rump or leg if you like a little fat.

800g (1lb 12oz) lamb, cut into 2cm (1in) cubes
vegetable oil, for the grill or pan
small amount of cumin and chilli flakes to garnish
8 skewers

MARINADE
1 tablespoon ground Sichuan peppercorns
1 tablespoon coriander (cilantro) powder

1 tablespoon cumin powder
3 tablespoons chilli flakes
2 garlic cloves, peeled and finely chopped
1 teaspoon salt
4 tablespoons lemon juice
50ml (1¾fl oz) vegetable oil
1 tablespoon caster (superfine) sugar
50ml (1¾fl oz) light soy sauce

In a bowl, mix together the marinade ingredients. Add the lamb, mix, cover and refrigerate overnight or for at least 2 hours.

Thread the lamb onto the skewers and cook them on a lightly oiled, preheated barbecue or in a frying pan on medium–high heat for around 5 minutes. Sprinkle over a little more cumin and chilli flakes and serve.

Makes 8

FISHY STICKS

SOY, GINGER AND SESAME CALAMARI SKEWERS

This is one of those hybrid Asian recipes that really can't be claimed exclusively by one country. I guess it has a leaning towards being Japanese more than anything else. It works so much better with fresh calamari, but if you can't get your hands on it, squid tubes will suffice.

700g (1lb 9oz) cleaned calamari
50ml (1¾fl oz) vegetable oil
10 skewers

MARINADE
75ml (2½fl oz) sweet soy sauce (ketjap manis)
75ml (2½fl oz) light soy sauce
3 tablespoons sesame oil

75ml (2½fl oz) rice wine vinegar
3cm (1½in) piece ginger, finely grated
2 tablespoons lime juice
2 spring onions (scallions), thinly sliced
2 tablespoons white sesame seeds, toasted
1 tablespoon black sesame seeds
2 large red chillies, seeded and thinly sliced

With a sharp knife, slice open the calamari and score it, making a crisscross pattern. Cut the calamari into roughly 5cm (2in) squares.

In a bowl, combine all the marinade ingredients, reserving a little of the spring onion and chilli for garnish. Add the calamari to the bowl, mix through, and leave to marinate in the refrigerator for at least 2 hours.

Thread the calamari onto the skewers, reserving the marinade liquid. Then pour the oil over the skewers. Place the skewers on a flat grill or chargrill, and cook over high heat, turning once, for about 2 minutes. Remove the cooked skewers and place them on a serving platter.

Heat a little of the leftover marinade in a saucepan and pour over the skewers.

Garnish with the remaining spring onion and chilli.

Serve with half a lime, and a salad of shredded carrot, bean sprouts, spring onion and spinach leaves.
Makes 10

CHILLED SESAME YELLOWFIN TUNA WITH DASHI MAYO

For me, almost nothing beats yellowfin or bluefin tuna. Its flavour is so fantastic that it's always best to keep it simple and show the fish the respect it thoroughly deserves. In this recipe we use Japanese seven spice, which has a really nice chilli kick.

400g (14oz) sashimi-grade yellowfin tuna, skinned and bloodline removed
½ teaspoon shichimi togarashi (Japanese seven spice)
2 tablespoons pickled ginger, finely chopped
1 tablespoon lime juice
3 tablespoons light soy sauce
2 tablespoons white sesame seeds
1 tablespoon rice wine vinegar
vegetable oil, for the grill or pan
12 two-pronged toothpicks

DASHI MAYO
1 egg yolk
2 tablespoons rice wine vinegar
200ml (7fl oz) vegetable oil
2 tablespoons sesame oil
1 tablespoon dashi
2 tablespoons light soy sauce
1 teaspoon caster (superfine) sugar
½ teaspoon ginger powder

GARNISH
½ teaspoon white sesame seeds
½ teaspoon black sesame seeds
1 teaspoon chives, chopped
½ teaspoon shichimi togarashi (Japanese seven spice)

To make the mayo, place the egg yolk and the vinegar in a food processor. Turn the processor on and slowly drizzle in the vegetable and sesame oils. Add the remaining ingredients and continue to process for a further minute. Place the mayo in a bowl, cover and refrigerate for later use.

To prepare the tuna, cut it into bite-sized cubes. In a bowl, combine the shichimi togarashi, ginger, lime juice, light soy sauce, sesame seeds and rice wine vinegar. Place the tuna into the bowl, mix together gently, cover and place in the refrigerator. Allow to marinate for 1 hour. Mix the garnish ingredients together.

Heat a frying pan or hot plate until really hot and cook the tuna quickly on two sides only—the tuna should still be quite raw. Allow to cool on a tray lined with absorbent paper in the refrigerator.

To serve, spoon a little of the dashi mayo onto a serving plate, and sprinkle the garnish over the mayo. Place a two-pronged toothpick into each piece of tuna and place them on the serving plate.

Makes 12

TIP
If you can't get shichimi togarashi (Japanese seven spice), use cayenne pepper instead.

PRAWN (SHRIMP) AND CHORIZO SKEWERS

I think a lot of us discovered and fell in love with chorizo the first time we ate paella. Chorizo would have to be one of the world's best sausages and, like most things porky, they go brilliantly with seafood.

12 prawns (shrimp), shelled and cleaned, tails left on
2 dried chorizo sausages, cut into 12 chunks
1 spring onion (scallions), cut into 12 pieces, about
    2cm (1in) long
vegetable oil, for the grill or pan
romesco sauce (see Sauces)
4 skewers

MARINADE
75ml (2½fl oz) olive oil
2 tablespoons sherry vinegar
2 garlic cloves, peeled and minced
¼ teaspoon chilli powder
1 teaspoon chilli flakes
½ teaspoon smoked paprika
½ teaspoon ground cumin
4 tablespoons coriander (cilantro), chopped
¼ teaspoon salt

To make the marinade, in a bowl, whisk together the oil, vinegar, garlic, chilli, paprika, cumin, coriander and salt. Add the prawns and chorizo, mix through, cover and marinate in the refrigerator for 30 minutes.

Thread a prawn, tail section first, on to the skewer, followed by a piece of chorizo and then the spring onion. Now thread the top of the prawn onto the skewer, so that it now surrounds the chorizo. Repeat the process until you have three prawns on each skewer. Reserve the marinade.

Cook the skewers on a lightly oiled chargrill or in a frying pan over medium–high heat, turning occasionally, and basting with the leftover marinade for around 5 minutes.

These skewers are great served with saffron rice and romesco sauce (see Sauces).

Makes 4

FIERY PRAWN (SHRIMP) SKEWERS

FIERY PRAWN (SHRIMP) SKEWERS

These guys are sure to set your mouth on fire! Make sure you have a cold drink—my preference is beer—on standby to dowse the flames.

24 medium-sized prawns (shrimp), shelled and
    cleaned, tails left on
vegetable oil, for the frying pan
small handful coriander (cilantro) extra (to garnish)
8 skewers

MARINADE
1 teaspoon chilli powder
½ teaspoon turmeric powder

1 teaspoon garam masala
3 tablespoons olive oil
½ teaspoon ground cumin
½ teaspoon ginger powder
1 garlic clove, peeled and finely chopped
1 small handful coriander (cilantro) leaves, chopped
2 large red chillies, seeded and diced
½ teaspoon salt

Place all of the marinade ingredients into a bowl and mix well. Add the prawns and mix well. Cover and refrigerate for at least 1 hour.

Thread three prawns onto each skewer. Preheat a chargrill or frying pan on high heat (if using a frying pan, add a little oil). Place the prawns on the grill or in a frying pan, reduce the heat a little, and cook for around 2 minutes each side.

Remove the prawns, and garnish with a little coriander and serve with lemon.
Makes 8

GARLIC AND CHILLI PRAWNS (SHRIMP) WITH LIME AIOLI

Who doesn't like garlic chilli prawns (shrimp)? This version is so quick and easy to put together you'll want to make them all the time.

24 prawns (shrimp), shelled and cleaned, tails left on
vegetable oil, for the grill
8 skewers

MARINADE
3 garlic cloves, finely chopped
1 large red chilli, finely chopped
3 tablespoons olive oil
1 tablespoon lemon juice
1 small handful flat-leaf parsley leaves, chopped
½ teaspoon salt

½ teaspoon freshly ground black pepper

LIME AIOLI
3 egg yolks
2 tablespoons lime juice
2 teaspoons Dijon mustard
250ml (9fl oz) olive oil
3 garlic cloves, finely chopped
1 teaspoon grated lime rind
salt and pepper, to taste

To make the aioli, place the egg yolks, lime juice and the mustard in a food processor. With the processor running slowly, gradually add the olive oil, and then add the garlic, lime rind, and salt and pepper to taste.

To prepare the marinade, in a bowl combine the garlic, chilli, oil, lemon juice, parsley, salt and pepper. Add the prawns and mix thoroughly. Cover and allow to marinate in the refrigerator for 30 minutes.

Thread three prawns onto each skewer and cook on a pre-heated chargrill, on high, for 2 minutes each side.

Serve with the lime aioli.
Makes 8

HIRAMASA KINGFISH WITH SOY, HONEY AND GINGER

Hiramasa kingfish is a fantastic fish. It's one of the best white fish that you can eat raw—it has the right firmness, as well as a great subtle flavour, and it's also fantastic just partially cooked.

1kg (2lb 4 oz) hiramasa kingfish, skinless and
     boneless
vegetable oil, for the grill or pan
15 skewers

MARINADE
3 tablespoons light soy sauce

3 tablespoons sweet soy sauce (ketjap manis)
2 tablespoons oyster sauce
3 tablespoons honey
1 teaspoon cracked black pepper
1 spring onion (scallions), chopped
1 garlic clove, minced
3cm (1½in) piece ginger, grated

Cut the kingfish into 3cm by 2cm (1½in by 1in) pieces.

Place all of the marinade ingredients in a bowl. Mix together thoroughly, add the kingfish, mix through, cover and allow to marinate in the refrigerator for 1 hour.

Thread three pieces of kingfish onto each skewer then cook on a lightly oiled flat grill or in a frying pan on high heat for around 1 minute each side. The kingfish should still be a little undercooked in the middle.

Makes 15

JAMÓN-WRAPPED PRAWNS (SHRIMP)

JAMÓN-WRAPPED PRAWNS (SHRIMP)

I really like the combination of pork and seafood. These Spanish-inspired prawns (shrimp) are a great addition to any cocktail party. This is another dish that looks great in shot glasses.

15 prawns (shrimp), shelled and cleaned,
   tails left on
8 jamón slices
1 pinch freshly ground black pepper
2 tablespoons flat-leaf parsley, chopped

2 tablespoons olive oil
vegetable oil, for the grill or pan
red pepper aioli (see Sauces)
15 toothpicks as skewers

Cut the jamón in half crossways and wrap it around a prawn. Put a toothpick through the thickest part of the prawn and also through the tail end. Put the black pepper, parsley and oil in a bowl, add the prawns and gently mix.

   Heat a little oil in a frying pan or on a flat grill and cook the prawns for around 2 minutes each side.

   Place the prawns on a serving plate with the aioli on the side, or spoon a little aioli into shot glasses and serve a prawn in each glass.

Makes 15

PRAWN (SHRIMP) WRAPPED SUGAR CANE

This is an extremely popular Vietnamese dish, and you'll find it pretty much in every market. The prawn (shrimp) meat is removed from the sugar cane, cut into strips and wrapped up in rice paper or lettuce leaves with fresh herbs. The version I make has tiny dried shrimps added.

700g (1lb 9oz) raw prawn (shrimp) meat
2 spring onions (scallions), chopped
2 garlic cloves, peeled and finely chopped
¼ teaspoon salt
½ teaspoon ground white pepper
1 teaspoon caster (superfine) sugar
2 tablespoons fish sauce

1 egg white
100g (3½oz) minced pork fat (ground pork fat)
100g (3½oz) dried shrimps, soaked in water for
   30 minutes, then drained
vegetable oil, for the grill or pan
12 sugar cane sticks cut into 10cm (4in) lengths
nuoc cham (see Sauces)

Put the prawn meat, spring onions, garlic, salt, pepper, sugar, fish sauce, egg white and pork fat into a food processor and process to a paste. Remove to a bowl, add the dried shrimps and mix through. Cover and allow to rest in the refrigerator for 30 minutes.

Divide the prawn mix into 12 portions. With wet hands, flatten a portion into the palm of your hand and then mould the prawn mix around the top two-thirds of the sugar cane. Continue until all the mixture has been used up.

Heat a small amount of oil on a flat grill or in a frying pan, and cook the sticks for around 5 minutes, turning occasionally.

Using a knife, remove the prawn mix from the sticks.

Serve with nuoc cham and, if you like, fresh herbs, such as Vietnamese mint, coriander, mint and Thai basil, as well as some rice paper and lettuce leaves.

Serves 4

SALMON, POTATO, LEMON AND ROSEMARY STICKS

Using rosemary as a skewer imparts a great flavour to the fish and it looks pretty good as well. Try to use the thick, older, woody stalks, so they don't go limp during cooking.

2 desiree potatoes, peeled and cut into 3cm (1½in) cubes (you'll need 16 pieces)

800g (1lb 12oz) salmon fillet, thick part, skinless and boneless

vegetable oil, for the grill or pan

8 hardy rosemary stalks for skewers

MARINADE

50ml (1¾fl oz) olive oil

2 garlic cloves, peeled and minced

2 tablespoons rosemary, chopped

½ small onion, peeled and finely diced

1 tablespoon red wine vinegar

2 teaspoons grated lemon rind

1 tablespoons lemon juice

¼ teaspoon salt

¼ teaspoon freshly ground black pepper

Put the potatoes in a saucepan, cover with water and put them on the stove, cook until tender. Remove from the water and allow them to cool.

In a bowl, mix together the marinade ingredients, and add the potatoes.

Cut the salmon into 3cm (1½in) cubes and add them to the bowl of marinade and potatoes, mix through, cover and leave to marinate for 1 hour in the refrigerator.

Meanwhile, remove all but the top 3cm (1½in) of rosemary sprigs from the rosemary stalks. Soak the stalks in water for 30 minutes so they won't burn. Remove the stalks from the water and shake off any excess water, and sharpen the stalk a little if possible.

Thread a piece of salmon then a piece of potato onto the stalk, and repeat the process until you have three pieces of salmon and two pieces of potato on each stalk.

Put a little oil onto a flat grill or in a frying pan that's been preheated to high. Cook the skewers, while basting with the remaining marinade, for around 3 minutes. The salmon should still be pink in the middle.

Remove from the heat and allow to rest for a few minutes before serving.

Serves 8

SOY AND FIVE SPICE RAINBOW TROUT STICKS WITH A BEAN SHOOT AND SESAME SALAD

Rainbow trout is a great fish that seems to live in the shadow of its way more popular cousin, salmon. The five spice adds a great flavour to the trout and the crunchy salad is the perfect partner.

800g (1lb 12oz) rainbow trout, skinless and boneless
vegetable oil, for the grill or pan
8 skewers

MARINADE
4cm (1½in) piece ginger, skinned and finely grated

100ml (3½fl oz) shaoxing (Chinese rice) wine
100ml (3½fl oz) sweet soy sauce (ketjap manis)
50ml (1¾fl oz) light soy sauce
2 tablespoons sesame oil
2 teaspoons five spice powder

Cut the rainbow trout into 2½cm (1in) cubes.

In a bowl, mix together the marinade ingredients. Add the rainbow trout, mix through, cover and place in the refrigerator to marinate for 2 hours.

Thread four pieces of rainbow trout onto each skewer. Put a little oil on a preheated hotplate or frying pan and cook the skewers for around 1½ minutes each side.

Serve with steamed jasmine rice and bean shoot and sesame salad (recipe on page 76).

Serves 4

BEAN SHOOT AND SESAME SALAD

200g (7oz) bean shoots
½ red onion, peeled and finely sliced
100g (3½oz) baby spinach, washed and sliced
1 small carrot, peeled and cut into fine batons
2 spring onions (scallions), finely sliced on an angle
2 tablespoons sesame seeds, toasted

GINGER DRESSING
1 egg yolk
2 teaspoons rice vinegar
2 teaspoons ginger powder
100ml (3½fl oz) vegetable oil
2 tablespoons sesame oil
2 tablespoons light soy sauce
1 tablespoon sweet soy sauce (ketjap manis)

To make the dressing, in a small mixing bowl, place the yolk, rice vinegar and ginger powder. Slowly drizzle in the oils while whisking, then add the soy sauces. Don't worry if the dressing splits, as it's not meant to have the consistency of mayonnaise.

Mix all of the salad ingredients together in a bowl, add a little of the dressing, and serve immediately.

SOY AND LEMONGRASS SALMON

Lemongrass gives any recipe a wonderful fragrant taste and it certainly comes through in this recipe. These are easy, tasty barbecue treats, but be careful not to overcook your salmon, as it can become quite dry.

500g (17½oz) salmon fillet, skinless and boneless
vegetable oil, for the grill or pan
1 bamboo skewer
4 lemongrass skewers, roughly 15cm (6in) long

MARINADE
2cm (1in) piece ginger, peeled and finely chopped

1 lemongrass stalk, white part only, finely chopped
30ml (1fl oz) lime juice
60ml (2fl oz) light soy sauce
30ml (1fl oz) vegetable oil
50ml (1¾fl oz) mirin
1 spring onion (scallions), chopped

Cut the salmon into uniformly sized pieces of about 40g (1½oz) each.

To make the marinade, combine the ginger, chopped lemongrass, lime juice, soy sauce, oil, mirin and spring onion in a bowl. Add the salmon pieces, mix through, cover and marinate for at least 1 hour.

Remove the salmon from the marinade. Using a bamboo skewer, pierce through the salmon lengthways. Remove the bamboo skewer and thread the lemongrass skewer through the hole. Put three pieces of salmon on each piece of lemongrass.

Cook the salmon over high heat, making sure not to overcook it, a little over a minute each side should do the trick. The salmon should still be quite pink in the middle.

Place the salmon on a serving plate and spoon over a little of the remaining marinade.

Makes 4

THE ULTIMATE SCALLOP BROCHETTE WITH PUREED PARSNIP AND PINE NUT SALAD

For me there is no better combo than scallops and prosciutto—I simply adore them together. Team them up with the truffle-scented parsnip puree and you've got a mouthful of heaven.

16 Canadian scallops
1 pinch table salt
1 pinch freshly ground black pepper
1 teaspoon truffle oil

1 teaspoon olive oil
vegetable oil, for the grill or pan
8 thin slices prosciutto
4 skewers

Place the scallops in a bowl with the salt, pepper, truffle oil and olive oil and mix through so the scallops are well coated.

Lay out the prosciutto and cut each slice in half crossways. Place a scallop on each prosciutto slice. Wrap the prosciutto around the scallop then thread the scallops onto the skewers, so you have four scallops on each skewer.

Place a little oil on a flat grill or in a frying pan and cook the scallop for around 1½ minutes each side —the scallops should be a little under-cooked in the middle.

Remove from the heat and place on top of the truffle and honey parsnip puree (recipe on page 81).

Top with the pine nut salad (recipe on page 81).

Serves 4

PUREED PARSNIP

750g (1lb 10oz) parsnips, peeled
100ml (3½fl oz) cream
2 tablespoons honey

3 tablespoons truffle oil
¼ teaspoon salt

Cut the parsnips in half. Check that the core isn't too woody—if it is, do your best to cut around it.

Cut the parsnip into cubes and place them in a saucepan, pour over enough water to cover. Bring the water to the boil, then turn down to a simmer and continue to cook for 15 minutes—you should be able to easily push a skewer into the parsnip when it is cooked.

Strain the parsnip and place it in a food processor with the remaining ingredients. Blend until you have a smooth puree.

PINE NUT SALAD

1 cup flat-leaf parsley leaves, shredded
100g (3½oz) pine nuts, toasted
100g (3½oz) currants

3 tablespoons extra virgin olive oil
1 tablespoon sherry vinegar
pinch of sea salt

Mix all the ingredients together in a bowl.

THE ULTIMATE SCALLOP
BROCHETTE, WITH PUREED PARSNIP
AND PINE NUT SALAD

BIRDY STICKS

CHICKEN SEKUWA

Ajaya and Kandel, both from Nepal, are great guys who work in the kitchen at Red Spice Road. They kept raving about these Nepalese chicken skewers so I got them to make some for me and they are extremely tasty. The boys tell me these skewers go well with tomato achar, so I've included a recipe (page 87).

750g (1lb 10oz) chicken breast or thigh, skinless
    and boneless
vegetable oil, for the grill or pan
10 skewers

MARINADE
2 red chillies, chopped
1 pinch coriander (cilantro) leaves, chopped

1 teaspoon curry powder
½ teaspoon ground nutmeg
½ teaspoon turmeric
1 lemongrass stalk, white part only, finely chopped
¼ teaspoon Sichuan pepper
1 garlic clove, peeled and chopped
1cm (½in) piece ginger, peeled and chopped
½ cup natural yoghurt

In a blender, process all the marinade ingredients into a smooth paste.

Place the chicken pieces in a bowl, pour over the marinade and mix, cover and leave to marinate in the refrigerator overnight or for at least 3 hours.

Thread the chicken pieces onto the skewers. When done, pour a little oil onto a grill and cook the skewers for around 10 minutes, turning occasionally until cooked through.

Makes 10

TOMATO ACHAR

5 ripe tomatoes
2 tablespoons vegetable oil
1 teaspoon cumin seeds
1 teaspoon mustard seeds
1 teaspoon Sichuan pepper
3 tablespoons vegetable oil
2 shallots (eschalots), peeled and sliced

3 small red chillies, chopped
3 garlic cloves, finely chopped
1cm (½in) piece ginger, peeled and finely chopped
2 tablespoons lime juice
1 teaspoons table salt
1 pinch mint leaves, chopped
1 pinch coriander (cilantro) leaves, chopped

Remove the eyes from the tomatoes. Cut a little cross at the top of each tomato, roll them in the 2 tablespoons of oil, then place them on a baking tray in a hot oven for around 15 minutes. Remove the tomatoes from the oven and remove the skins, then roughly chop the tomatoes.

Dry-fry the cumin seeds, mustard seeds and Sichuan pepper in a frying pan, and when toasted, grind in a spice grinder, food processor or mortar and pestle. Heat the remaining vegetable oil in a saucepan, add the shallots, chillies, garlic and ginger, and cook while stirring for around 1 minute. Add the ground spices. Add the tomatoes, lime juice, salt, mint and coriander and continue to cook while stirring for 2 minutes.

Pour into a bowl and allow to cool.

Makes about 500ml (17fl oz)

CHICKEN TIKKA WITH CUCUMBER SALAD AND RIATA

Chicken tikka is an Indian favourite. It goes really well with this refreshing cucumber salad and the cooling riata.

4 chicken breasts, skinless and boneless,
    cut into 3cm (1½in) cubes
vegetable oil, for the grill
riata (see Sauces)
4 long skewers

MARINADE
200g (7oz) natural yoghurt
3 tablespoons tikka curry paste
1 tablespoon lemon juice

SALAD
1 Lebanese cucumber, peeled and cut into cubes
250g (9oz) cherry tomatoes, halved
1 handful coriander (cilantro) leaves
1 medium-sized red onion, peeled and finely sliced
1 handful mint leaves, shredded
2 tablespoons lemon juice
2 tablespoons olive oil
1 pinch salt

In a bowl, mix together the yoghurt, tikka paste and the lemon juice. Add the chicken, mix well, cover and leave to marinate in the refrigerator for at least 2 hours.

Thread the chicken onto four skewers, cover and place them in the refrigerator for later use.

In the meantime, make the riata (see Sauces).

Heat a little oil on a medium-hot grill and cook the chicken, turning regularly, for around 10 minutes.

While the chicken is cooking, make the salad by combining all the ingredients in a bowl, mix well and divide among four serving plates. Place a cooked chicken skewer on top and spoon over some riata (page 180).

Serves 4

TIP
You'll find tikka paste in most
supermarkets.

CHICKEN LIVER, SAGE AND BEETROOT SKEWERS

I generally love Thai street food but the one thing I can't stomach from a street cart is a chicken liver skewer. They're always overcooked and that's not a good thing when it comes to chicken livers. And the major problem for me is that they really do look like beef so I always make the same mistake and keep ordering them. The skewers described here, on the other hand, are quite tasty—but please make sure you don't overcook them.

24 chicken livers, cleaned
16 sage leaves
8 baby beetroot, cooked, peeled and cut in half
vegetable oil, for the grill or pan
8 skewers

MARINADE
2 tablespoons balsamic vinegar
5 tablespoons olive oil
2 garlic cloves, peeled and finely chopped
½ teaspoon salt
¼ teaspoon freshly ground black pepper
¼ teaspoon brown sugar

In a bowl, mix together the marinade ingredients. Add the livers, cover and marinate in the refrigerator for 30 minutes.

On a skewer, thread a chicken liver, sage leaf then a beetroot half, and repeat the process, and finally finish off with a chicken liver: there should be three chicken livers on each skewer.

Heat a little oil in a frying pan or on a flat grill, and cook on high heat for about 1½ minutes each side. Allow the livers to rest for a few minutes before serving.

To serve, heat a little of the marinade and pour it over the skewers, and accompany with a rocket and red onion salad.

Makes 8

CHICKEN YAKITORI

CHICKEN YAKITORI

I fell in love with yakitori—a Japanese classic—the first time I tried it. You could say it was love at first bite. My wife and I can never pass it up when we go to a Japanese restaurant.

600g (1lb 5oz) chicken thigh meat, skinless and
    boneless
2 spring onions (scallions), trimmed and cut into
    2cm (1in) long pieces
1 extra spring onion (scallion), trimmed and sliced
    on an angle (for garnish)
8 skewers

MARINADE
50ml (1¾fl oz) light soy sauce
50ml (1¾fl oz) sake
30ml (1fl oz) mirin
1 teaspoon dashi
1 pinch ground white pepper
2cm (1in) knob of ginger, grated finely then
    squeezed for the juice
1 teaspoon cornflour (cornstarch)

Place the soy, sake, mirin, dashi, white pepper and ginger juice into a small saucepan. Bring to the boil and then simmer for 1 minute. Mix the cornflour with a little water and mix until it dissolves. Add the cornflour mix to the saucepan while whisking, and continue to whisk for a further 1 minute. Set aside to cool.

Meanwhile, cut the chicken thigh into small pieces and place in a bowl. When the marinade is cool enough, pour a little more than half over the chicken, mix, cover and refrigerate for at least 30 minutes.

Thread a piece of chicken onto a skewer followed by a spring onion piece, and repeat the process until you have three pieces of chicken and two pieces of spring onion on each skewer.

Heat a little oil either in a frying pan or on the flat grill of a barbecue. Cook the skewers, tuning once, for around 5 to 6 minutes or until cooked through.

Transfer the skewers to a serving plate, drizzle over the remaining marinade and top with spring onions.
Makes 8

TIP
If you can't get hold of dashi, simply
omit it from the recipe. If you can't
get hold of mirin, use 1 tablespoon of
caster (superfine) sugar instead.

GRILLED ISSAN CHICKEN

Yet another Thai street favourite. Thais use a unique two-pronged bamboo apparatus to secure the chicken, but I've just used large metal skewers. These skewers are usually cooked on a wire rack over flames, but we'll make do with the chargrill section of a barbecue.

4 chicken Marylands (thigh with drumstick
     attached)
sweet chilli sauce (see Sauces)
8 large metal skewers

MARINADE
2 garlic cloves, roughly chopped
1 lemongrass stalk, white part only, finely chopped
5 coriander roots, roughly chopped
1cm (½in) piece turmeric, peeled and chopped
1 tablespoon white peppercorns
40g (1½oz) palm sugar, shaved
50ml (1¾fl oz) fish sauce
50ml (1¾fl oz) vegetable oil

In a mortar and pestle, add the garlic, lemongrass, coriander root, turmeric, peppercorns and the palm sugar. Pound all the ingredients until a paste forms. Add the fish sauce and the vegetable oil, and stir until combined.

Place the chicken Marylands in a bowl and pour over the marinade. Cover, and marinate overnight or for at least 3 hours.

Skewer each chicken Maryland with two large metal skewers and place on the chargrill on medium heat, and close the lid on the barbecue if there is one. Turn the skewers every so often, taking care not to burn them. Cook for around 20 minutes or until cooked through.

Serve with sweet chilli sauce and a fresh bean sprout, coriander (cilantro), mint and cucumber salad.
Serves 4

HOISIN AND GINGER DUCK SKEWERS

I love the taste of hoisin sauce, and it's the perfect foil for duck. If you can't get your hands on duck breasts, simply substitute chicken breast—if you are using chicken, make sure you cook it through.

4 duck breasts, skin removed
2 spring onions (scallions), cleaned and cut into
    2cm (¾in) batons
vegetable oil, for the grill or pan
1 extra tablespoon hoisin sauce, mixed with
    a little water
1 tablespoon spring onions (scallions), chopped
8 skewers

MARINADE
4 tablespoons hoisin sauce
½ garlic clove, peeled and finely chopped
2 tablespoons sesame oil
2 tablespoons shaoxing (Chinese rice) wine
1 large red chilli, seeded and finely chopped
1cm (½in) piece ginger, peeled and finely grated
2 tablespoons soy sauce
2 tablespoons sesame seeds, toasted

Cut the duck breast into eight pieces per breast and place in a bowl. Add all of the marinade ingredients. Mix together well, cover and refrigerate for at least 2 hours.

Put four pieces of duck on each skewer, separating each piece of duck with a spring onion baton.

Pour a little oil onto the flat grill of the barbecue or in a frying pan and cook the skewers for around 2 minutes each side (if using chicken, cook for around 5 minutes each side)—you want the duck to be a little undercooked.

Rest the skewers for a few minutes and serve garnished with the extra hoisin and the chopped spring onion.
Makes 8

INDIAN-INSPIRED TURKEY SKEWERS

We generally think turkey only when Christmas or Thanksgiving rolls around, which is unfortunate because it has a great flavour that we should be enjoying all year round.

600g (1lb 5oz) turkey breast meat, cut into
   3cm (1½in) pieces
vegetable oil, for the grill or pan
riata (see Sauces)
4 large skewers

MARINADE
1½ teaspoons ground cumin
1½ teaspoons ground coriander (cilantro)
1 teaspoon ground turmeric
1 teaspoon ground cardamom
½ teaspoon saffron powder
1 teaspoon chilli powder
1 handful mint leaves, chopped finely
1 handful coriander (cilantro) leaves, chopped finely
200ml (7fl oz) natural yoghurt
50ml (1¾fl oz) vegetable oil
½ teaspoon salt

In a bowl, mix together all the marinade ingredients. Add the turkey, cover and allow to marinate in the refrigerator for 1 hour.

Thread the turkey onto the skewers and cook over high heat on a lightly oiled grill or in a frying pan.

Serve with riata, steamed rice (preferably basmati) and a tomato, cucumber and mint salad.

Serves 4

JOOJEH KABAB (PERSIAN LEMON AND SAFFRON CHICKEN KEBABS)

Years ago, I worked with a Persian chef who sometimes made these great-tasting kebabs for us. It was always a treat for everyone in the kitchen. I've since learned that traditionally they are served with tomato and peppers that have also been chargrilled on skewers, so I have included a recipe for you below.

4 large chicken thighs, skinless and boneless
   cut into 3cm (1½in) pieces
vegetable oil, for the grill or pan
½ teaspoon salt
¼ teaspoon freshly ground black pepper
4 long skewers

MARINADE
1 onion, peeled and chopped as fine as you can
½ teaspoon smoked paprika
¼ teaspoon cayenne pepper
1 teaspoon saffron threads
4 tablespoons lemon juice
3 tablespoons olive oil

For the marinade, in a mortar and pestle, add the onion, paprika, cayenne and saffron, and pound to a rough paste. Add the lemon juice and the olive oil, and pour into a bowl. Add the chicken pieces to the marinade and mix well; cover and allow to marinate in the refrigerator overnight.

Thread the chicken onto the four skewers, season them with the salt and pepper, and cook on a hot chargrill, turning and basting regularly for around 10 minutes.

Serves 4

TOMATO KEBABS

4 large green chillies (try to buy the ones that aren't
   too hot)
12 ripe cherry tomatoes

2 tablespoons olive oil
pinch of salt
pinch of ground black pepper

Cut off the ends and the tips of the chillies and discard. Cut the chillies into three evenly sized pieces, and put them in a bowl with the tomatoes, oil, salt and pepper.

Thread four tomatoes and three chilli pieces onto each skewer. Cook each skewer on a hot chargrill for around 1½ minutes each side.

Serve the chicken and the tomato skewers together, with rice, flat-leaf parsley and lemon.

Serve with couscous, pita bread and some yoghurt.

Serves 4

MALAYSIAN CHICKEN SATAY

Malaysia is incredibly famous for its satays, and sometimes you'll find whole streets selling them. That's why there are so many different Malaysian satays out there in recipe land, so I thought I might as well throw my version into the mix as well.

750g (1lb 10oz) chicken thighs, skinless and boneless cut into 1½cm (¾in) pieces
vegetable oil, for the grill or pan
3 tablespoons peanuts, roasted and ground
20 skewers

MARINADE
2 lemongrass stalks, white part only, finely chopped
3 garlic cloves, peeled and finely chopped
2cm (¾in) piece galangal, finely grated
2cm (¾in) piece ginger, finely grated
75g (2½oz) caster (superfine) sugar
1 tablespoon ground turmeric powder
50ml (1¾fl oz) light soy sauce
50ml (1¾fl oz) vegetable oil

For the marinade, in a blender, puree the lemongrass, garlic, galangal, ginger, caster sugar, turmeric powder, soy sauce and the vegetable oil.

Transfer the marinade to a bowl, add the chicken and the peanuts, and mix together well. Cover and refrigerate overnight.

Thread three or four pieces of chicken onto one end of the skewers. Chargrill over high heat for around 5–6 minutes, turning occasionally. Serve with spicy peanut sauce (recipe on page 106).

Makes 20

SPICY PEANUT SAUCE

100ml (3½fl oz) vegetable oil

8 large dried chillies, soaked, stems removed, chopped

3cm (1½in) piece galangal, finely grated

3cm (1½in) piece ginger, finely grated

2 lemongrass stalks, white part only, finely chopped

4 shallots (eschalots), peeled and sliced

1 tablespoon belacan (shrimp paste)

1½ cups roasted peanuts, finely ground

3 garlic cloves, peeled and finely chopped

100g (3½oz) caster (superfine) sugar

250ml (9fl oz) water

100ml (3½fl oz) light soy sauce

Heat the oil in a wok or frying pan and fry the chillies, galangal, ginger, lemongrass, shallots and shrimp paste for 2 to 3 minutes. Transfer to a blender and blend into a smooth paste. Transfer to a saucepan, add the rest of the ingredients, bring to the boil and then reduce to a simmer. Continue to cook while stirring occasionally for 45 minutes.

Makes just over 500ml (17fl oz)

PORTUGUESE-STYLE CHICKEN SKEWERS

The Portuguese are known for their incredible barbecued chicken, so including a recipe was a must. And indeed these skewers are awesome on the barbecue. Just fiery enough not to blow your head off, they have a fantastic flavour.

1kg (2lb 4oz) chicken thighs, skinless and boneless
50ml (1¾fl oz) vegetable oil
1 lemon, to serve
10 skewers

MARINADE
3 garlic cloves, peeled and finely chopped
3 tablespoons smoked paprika
1 large red chilli, minced
1 teaspoon ground cumin
juice and rind of 1 lemon
3 tablespoons olive oil
½ cup coriander (cilantro) leaves, chopped
½ cup flat-leaf parsley leaves, chopped
1 teaspoon salt

Cut the chicken thighs into roughly 3cm (1½in) cubes.

Place all the marinade ingredients into a mixing bowl, add the chicken and mix well. Cover and allow to marinate in the refrigerator overnight.

Thread four pieces of chicken onto each skewer and oil each of them. Preheat your barbecue and grill the skewers over high heat, turning frequently, for around 10 minutes.

Serve with a squeeze of lemon and a simple lettuce, tomato, onion and cucumber salad.

Makes 10

SHISH TAOUK (LEBANESE CHICKEN SKEWERS)

This recipe comes from a friend's mother. And, of course, like any son he swears that his mother's are the best. These are great with tabouleh and fresh pita bread.

4 chicken breasts, skinless and boneless
1 green capsicum (bell pepper), cut into
   2cm (¾in) cubes
1 onion, peeled and cut into 2cm (¾in) cubes
8 small button mushrooms
vegetable oil, for the grill or pan
4 long skewers

MARINADE
2 garlic cloves, peeled and finely chopped
50ml (1¾fl oz) olive oil
3 tablespoons lemon juice
200ml (7fl oz) natural yoghurt
4 tablespoons tomato paste
2 tablespoons sumac
2 tablespoons dried thyme
1 tablespoon paprika
1 teaspoon black pepper
1 teaspoon salt
1 teaspoon allspice powder

In a bowl, mix together the marinade ingredients.

Cut the chicken into 2½cm (1in) cubes, and add the chicken to the marinade. Cover and marinate in the refrigerator for at least 3 hours.

Thread the chicken onto four long skewers with two pieces each of the onion, green capsicum and the mushrooms on each skewer. Cook the skewers in a lightly oiled frying pan or on a grill, turning occasionally, for around 8–10 minutes.

Serve with tabouleh and pita bread.

Serves 4

FIVE SPICE QUAIL WITH VIETNAMESE SLAW

Quail and five spice are a well-known combination. At Red Spice Road we do other versions of this dish, where we usually flour and fry the quail. At home it's easier to skewer them and throw them on the barbecue.

4 jumbo quails

4 long skewers

MARINADE

5 tablespoons shaoxing (Chinese rice) wine

5 tablespoons light soy sauce

1 tablespoon sesame oil

2 tablespoons vegetable oil

½ teaspoon chilli powder

1 tablespoon caster (superfine) sugar

1 teaspoon five spice powder

2cm (1in) piece of ginger, finely grated

VIETNAMESE SLAW

1 cup Savoy cabbage, finely shredded

½ Lebanese cucumber, peeled and sliced

1 small carrot, peeled and cut into thin batons

3 shallots (eschalots), peeled and sliced

2 red radish, cut in half and sliced

1 large red chilli, halved, seeded and sliced

10 mint leaves, shredded

½ cup coriander (cilantro) leaves

15 Vietnamese mint leaves

5 tablespoons peanuts, chopped (optional)

4 tablespoons crispy fried shallots (optional)

75ml (2½fl oz) nuoc cham (see Sauces)

Using a sharp knife remove the legs and the breasts from the quail. Also remove the thighbones from the legs: you can do this by holding the end of the bone and pulling down on the meat. You can then twist the bone off at the knee joint.

Combine all the marinade ingredients in a bowl and mix together thoroughly. Add the quail pieces, cover and refrigerate for 2 to 3 hours.

Thread four quail pieces onto each skewer—I like to keep the breasts and legs on separate skewers, but you can mix them if you like. Cook the skewers on the chargrill over high heat, turning occasionally for around 5 to 6 minutes. When they are cooked, remove from the grill and set aside to rest in a warm place for 5 minutes.

To make the slaw, combine all the ingredients in a bowl, add the nuoc cham, and mix together

Serves 4

FIVE SPICE QUAIL WITH VIETNAMESE SLAW

SUMATRAN MINCED DUCK SATAY

I came across this recipe in a book, but I always seem to change a couple of elements. These satays are tasty and, because they feature minced duck, are a little different as well.

600g (1lb 5oz) duck meat
1 teaspoon salt
2 lemongrass stalks, white part only, finely chopped
200g (7oz) chicken mince
8 kaffir lime leaves, finely sliced (needle-like)
1 handful coriander (cilantro), chopped
vegetable oil, for the grill or pan
10 wooden chopsticks, soaked in water overnight

SPICE PASTE
2 cloves
1 tablespoon cumin seeds

1 tablespoon coriander (cilantro) seeds
1 teaspoon turmeric powder
¼ teaspoon ground cinnamon
10 cashew nuts
4 garlic cloves, peeled and chopped
3 bullet chillies, seeded and chopped
6 shallots (eschalots), peeled and chopped
1½ tablespoons caster (superfine) sugar
3cm (1½in) piece ginger, peeled and chopped
1 teaspoon belacan (shrimp paste)
2 tablespoons vegetable oil

To make the spice paste, grind the cloves, cumin seeds and coriander seeds in a mortar and pestle. Put them in a food processor with all the other paste ingredients. Blend until you have an even smooth paste. Heat a little oil in a wok or saucepan, add the paste and cook for around 5 minutes. Set aside to cool.

Put the duck meat, salt and lemongrass in the food processor and blend until reasonably smooth.

In a bowl, mix together the spice paste, duck mixture, chicken mince, lime leaves and coriander. Mix together thoroughly.

Mould the mixture around the thin end of the chopsticks to form a sausage-like shape. Cook the sticks with a little oil on a flat grill or in a frying pan over high heat on all sides for about 5 minutes.

Makes 10

THAI GRILLED CHICKEN SATAY

I might be a bit biased because I go to Thailand so much, but these are probably my favourite satay and they are a little bit easier to make than the Malaysian version in this chapter. They're a great late night snack after a night out.

500g (17½oz) chicken breast, skinless and cut into
    strips crossways
vegetable oil, to baste
10 bamboo skewers, soaked in water overnight

MARINADE
1 teaspoon cumin seeds, roasted
2 teaspoons coriander (cilantro) seeds, roasted

3cm (1½in) piece fresh turmeric, peeled and grated
3cm (1½in) piece ginger, peeled and grated
2 garlic cloves, peeled and finely chopped
3 shallots (eschalots), peeled and chopped
2 tablespoons fish sauce
3 tablespoons vegetable oil
2 tablespoons caster (superfine) sugar

In a mortar and pestle, pound the cumin and coriander seeds, turmeric, ginger, garlic and shallots into a fine paste. Add the fish sauce, oil and sugar. Pour the marinade into a mixing bowl and add the chicken. Cover and refrigerate for at least 2 hours.

Thread the chicken strips onto the skewers. Brush the chicken with a little oil and cook them on the chargrill, turning occasionally, for around 4 minutes.

Makes 10

VEGGIE STICKS

PATATAS BRAVAS

My favourite restaurant in Melbourne is a Spanish place called Movida Aqui, and they do a great version of this dish. It would have to be one of the most popular tapas dishes of all time. Here's my version.

4 sebago potatoes, peeled and cut into 2½cm (1in) pieces
750ml (26fl oz) olive oil
½ teaspoon sea salt
1 teaspoon smoked paprika
15 to 18 small skewers or toothpicks

TABASCO AIOLI
red pepper aioli (see Sauces)
tabasco sauce, to taste

For the dressing, mix the tabasco into the aioli and set aside.

Put the potatoes in a saucepan, cover with salted water and bring to the boil. Turn down to a simmer and cook until the potatoes are tender. Drain the potatoes, put them in the refrigerator, uncovered, and allow them to cool.

Heat the oil in a large saucepan or a wok. Check to see if the oil is hot enough by dropping in a little piece of potato—if the potato sizzles, the oil is ready. Fry the potatoes, in batches if necessary, until they're golden and crispy. Toss the potatoes in the paprika and the sea salt.

Drizzle the tabasco aioli over the potatoes, and put a toothpick or small skewer in each potato.
Makes 15 to 20

TIP

When deep-frying at home please be very careful as it can be dangerous— always use a larger saucepan or wok than you think you need to avoid a boil-over.

BASIL AND GARLIC VEG STICKS

These multicoloured skewers are the perfect vegetarian barbecue treat. Not only are they great to look at, they also have lovely sweet and sour flavours.

2 medium-sized desiree potatoes, cut into
   2cm (¾in) cubes
1 red onion, peeled and cut into 2cm (¾in) chunks
12 button mushrooms
12 cherry or pear tomatoes
2 small zucchini (courgettes), cut into 12 pieces
6 small yellow squash, cut in half
1 large red capsicum (bell pepper), cut into
   12 pieces
vegetable oil, for the grill or pan
romesco sauce (see Sauces)
6 large skewers

MARINADE
50ml (1¾fl oz) olive oil
2 tablespoons seeded mustard
3 tablespoons balsamic vinegar
1 garlic clove, peeled and finely chopped
½ cup basil, finely chopped
2 tablespoons honey
½ teaspoon sea salt
¼ teaspoon freshly ground black pepper

Cook the potatoes in salted water until tender. Drain and let them cool down.

In a bowl, mix together the marinade ingredients. Place the potatoes in a bowl with the other vegetables, and pour over the marinade. Mix through carefully, cover and refrigerate for 1 hour.

Thread the vegetables onto the skewers, alternating them by colour.

Cook the skewers on a lightly oiled grill or in a frying pan on a high heat for around 8 minutes, or until the onion is cooked.

Serve with romesco sauce.

Makes 6

CORN AND GREEN ONION FRITTERS

These fritters are extremely popular at Red Spice Road. In fact, I promised one of our good customers that I would include them in the book—actually they threatened that they wouldn't buy it otherwise.

3 cups corn kernels

2 garlic cloves, peeled and minced

3 large red chillies, seeded and finely chopped

¼ teaspoon ground white pepper

1 handful coriander (cilantro) leaves, chopped

1 handful mint leaves, chopped

1 small handful Thai basil leaves

½ teaspoon ginger powder

6 kaffir lime leaves, finely sliced

4 tablespoons light soy sauce

3 eggs

3 spring onions (scallions), chopped

125g (4oz) self-raising (self-rising) flour

½ teaspoon baking powder

750ml (26fl oz) vegetable oil

sweet chilli sauce (see Sauces)

20 two-pronged skewers

Place half the corn, garlic, red chillies, pepper, coriander, mint, basil, ginger powder, kaffir lime leaves and soy sauce in a food processor. Blend and pour into a mixing bowl.

   Add the remaining corn, eggs, spring onions and the self-raising flour, and mix well with a wooden spoon.

   Heat the oil in a wok or a large saucepan to around 170°C (335°F).

   Using two spoons, shape the mixture into ovals, and drop them into the oil. Fry in batches until golden brown (around 5 minutes). Place a two-pronged skewer in each fritter and serve with sweet chilli sauce

Makes around 20

TIP

Fresh corn is best but canned corn
kernels are OK to use, too.

HALOUMI AND MEDITERRANEAN VEGETABLE KEBABS

HALOUMI AND MEDITERRANEAN VEGETABLE KEBABS

Haloumi is one of those cheeses that's great for grilling or frying and its mild flavour means it teams beautifully with the vegetables. These kebabs go beautifully with tzatziki.

400g (14oz) haloumi
1 medium-sized red onion, peeled
100g (3½oz) button mushrooms
1 medium-sized zucchini (courgette)
2 red capsicum (bell peppers)
200g (7oz) cherry tomatoes
vegetable oil, for the grill or pan
tzatziki (see Sauces)
10 skewers

MARINADE
1 garlic clove, peeled and finely chopped
2 tablespoons oregano, chopped
1 teaspoon finely grated lemon rind
½ teaspoon sea salt
3 tablespoons olive oil
¼ teaspoon ground white pepper

Cut the haloumi into roughly 2cm (1in) cubes. Cut the onion, mushrooms, zucchini and red peppers into pieces of a similar size to the haloumi.

Place the vegetables in a bowl with the marinade ingredients, mix well and leave to marinate for 2 hours.

Thread the vegetables and the haloumi onto the skewers, alternating colours, onto the 10 skewers.

Heat the barbeque plate or a frying pan, add a little oil and cook the skewers, turning occasionally until the cheese turns a golden colour.

Serve with tzatziki and some pita bread.

Makes 10

JERK VEGETABLE STICKS

Jerk is a Caribbean term that refers to the process of spicing food. It's pretty fiery, so you need to be able to handle a decent chilli kick to enjoy these sticks. Of course, if you can't handle the heat, just reduce the amount of chilli and cayenne pepper.

12 button mushrooms

12 cauliflower flowerets, cooked

12 cherry tomatoes

12 firm tofu cubes

1 large green capsicum (bell pepper), cut into
    12 pieces

2 small zucchini (courgettes), cut into 12 pieces

vegetable oil, for the grill or pan

12 skewers

MARINADE

100ml (3½fl oz) light soy sauce

75ml (2½fl oz) red wine vinegar

50ml (1¾fl oz) vegetable oil

50g (1¾oz) brown sugar

2 tablespoons dried thyme

½ teaspoon ground clove

¼ teaspoon cayenne pepper

½ teaspoon ground allspice

¼ teaspoon nutmeg

3 small red chillies, finely chopped

In a bowl, mix together all the marinade ingredients.

Add the vegetables and tofu, mix through, cover and refrigerate for 1 hour.

Thread one piece of each vegetable and a piece of tofu onto the skewers, and cook on a lightly oiled hot barbecue or in a frying pan for around 5 minutes.

Makes 12

ROSEMARY POTATO SKEWERS WITH MELTED TALLEGIO

Tallegio is an Italian soft-rind cheese that goes remarkably well with potato and rosemary. These skewers are really quite easy to make and are great on their own or as an accompaniment to beef or lamb.

4 medium-sized desiree potatoes, peeled and cut
    into 3cm (1½in) chunks
100g (3½oz) tallegio
2 tablespoons rosemary sprigs, chopped, extra
vegetable oil, for the grill or pan
4 skewers

MARINADE
3 tablespoons olive oil
1 garlic clove, peeled and finely chopped
1 teaspoon grated lemon rind
2 tablespoons rosemary sprigs, chopped
½ teaspoon salt
¼ teaspoon freshly ground black pepper

Put the potatoes in a saucepan, cover with water and cook until tender. Drain, and allow to cool slightly, then thread them onto the skewers.

In a bowl, mix together the marinade ingredients.

Brush the skewers with the rosemary mixture and place them onto a hot chargrill, turning them occasionally. Continue to brush the skewers with the rosemary mixture while they are cooking, and cook for around 10 minutes.

Remove the skewers from the chargrill and place them on a heatproof tray. Place some tallegio on top then sprinkle over the rosemary.

Place the tray in a hot oven, preheated to 220°C (420°F), for a few minutes to melt the tallegio.

Remove from the oven and serve immediately.

Serves 4

SWEET POTATO, ASPARAGUS AND BOCCONCINI STICKS

These babies are great, because you can plate them up well ahead of time, as they are served at room temperature. Asparagus is one of my favourite vegetables and is a must-eat in spring when it's in season and in its eating prime. I love asparagus so much that, years ago when I was asked by a previous boss why I was using it out of season, my response was that it was in season in Peru, which was where I was getting it from.

1 large sweet potato, peeled and cut into 12 3cm (1½in) thick pieces
olive oil, extra
12 baby bocconcini balls, or 3 normal-sized mozzarella balls, cut into quarters
12 asparagus tips, the top 4cm (1½in) only
1 teaspoon chilli flakes

1 teaspoon coriander (cilantro) seeds
pinch of salt and pepper, extra
1 small handful basil leaves, finely chopped
¼ teaspoon freshly ground black pepper
½ teaspoon sea salt
100ml (3fl oz) extra virgin olive oil
12 small skewers

Place the sweet potato pieces in a bowl, and toss with a little olive oil. Put the sweet potato on an oiled baking tray and roast them in a hot oven, preheated to 220°C (420°F), for about 15 minutes, turning occasionally and making sure the pieces don't start to fall apart. Remove from the oven and allow to cool.

Put the chilli flakes, coriander seeds and a pinch of pepper and salt in a mortar and pestle, and grind them until they are quite fine. Toss the sweet potato in the ground spices.

In a bowl, mix together the basil, some olive oil and some salt and pepper. Add the bocconcini and toss.

In a saucepan, bring some salted water to the boil, add the asparagus and cook for 1½ minutes. Remove the asparagus and refresh in cold water.

Thread a piece of the bocconcini onto a skewer, followed by the asparagus and finally the sweet potato. Repeat for all 12 skewers.

Makes 12

TOFU, SHIITAKE MUSHROOM, WASABI AND GREEN ONION STICKS

Really tasty, Japanese-inspired vegetarian sticks for the barbecue. Your vego friends will be impressed.

500g (17½oz) firm tofu cut into 2½cm (1in) cubes
3 spring onions (scallions), cut into 3cm (1½in) lengths
24 small shiitake mushroom caps
vegetable oil, for the grill or pan
3 tablespoons sesame seeds, toasted
6 skewers

MARINADE
50ml (1¾fl oz) light soy sauce
1 teaspoon wasabi paste
1 teaspoon caster (superfine) sugar
1 tablespoon sesame oil
5cm (2in) piece ginger, finely grated

For the marinade, in a bowl, mix together the soy, wasabi, sugar and sesame oil. Squeeze the juice out of the ginger into the bowl, and discard the grated ginger.

Add the tofu and the shiitakes to the marinade, mix through, cover and allow to marinate in the refrigerator for 1 hour.

Thread one piece each of the tofu, shiitake and spring onions, and repeat so you have four pieces of each on each skewer. Reserve the marinade liquid.

Heat a little oil on a flat grill or in a frying pan and cook the skewers for around 6 minutes, turning occasionally. When cooked, sprinkle the skewers with the toasted sesame seeds.

Serve the skewers by themselves or with a fennel, radish, green onion and seaweed salad, using the remaining marinade as the dressing.

Makes 6

MUSHROOM, EGGPLANT (AUBERGINE) AND OLIVE SKEWERS

These are hearty vegetarian skewers. They go really well with salsa verde, and silky smooth potato puree or soft polenta.

2 eggplant (aubergine), cut into 2½–3cm (1–1½in) pieces
18 button mushrooms, halved
vegetable oil, for the grill or pan
salsa verde (see Sauces)
12 skewers

MARINADE
3 tablespoons balsamic vinegar
2 garlic cloves, peeled and crushed
½ teaspoon fine sea salt
¼ teaspoon freshly ground black pepper
10 sage leaves, finely chopped
75ml (2½fl oz) olive oil

Place the vegetables and the marinade ingredients into a bowl, mix together, cover and marinate for 30 minutes.

Thread three mushroom pieces, alternating with three eggplant pieces, onto each skewer.

Cook the skewers on an oiled flat grill or on a chargrill, turning occasionally for around 8 minutes. Before you serve, make sure the eggplant is cooked through.

Serve with salsa verde.

Makes 12

WATERMELON, FETA AND OLIVE

Watermelon and feta have a long-lasting friendship that works well. As long as you get your hands on good-quality feta and a juicy, full-flavoured watermelon, there really is no need to do anything much to them. In this case, simple is best.

8 mint leaves
15 pitted kalamata olives
15 squares watermelon, in 3cm (1½in) cubes
30ml (1fl oz) arak
3 tablespoons extra virgin olive oil

400g (14oz) sheep's milk feta
2 tablespoons sumac
3 tablespoons thyme leaves, chopped
olive oil, extra (to dress the skewers)
15 small skewers

Roll up a small piece of mint and push it into the olive cavity.

In a bowl, mix together the watermelon and arak, and leave to stand for 5 minutes. Drain off any excess arak.

In another bowl, mix together the olive oil and feta. Remove the feta and sprinkle it with the sumac and thyme.

Thread a piece each of watermelon, feta and an olive onto small skewers. If desired, drizzle over a little more extra virgin olive oil.

Makes 15

TIP
Arak is an aniseed-flavoured Middle Eastern spirit. If you can't find it, just use ouzo.

RETRO STICKS

CHEESE AND BEER FONDUE

Not knowing much about fondues—well, not much being nothing at all—forced me to go to my trusty sidekick, Adam, for advice to get some basic ideas about what goes on in fondue land. And that's how we came up with this recipe—beer and cheese combined in the one pot. Genius! So we gave it a try and it wasn't half bad.

200g (7oz) Gruyère cheese, grated
200g (7oz) aged cheddar cheese, grated
200g (7oz) Gouda cheese, grated
200ml (7fl oz) beer, at room temperature

2 tablespoons plain (all-purpose) flour
1 tablespoon Dijon mustard
¼ teaspoon freshly ground black pepper

In a bowl, add the grated cheeses with the plain flour. Mix well so that the cheese is coated with flour.

Pour the beer into a large saucepan and bring it to a simmer over high heat. Reduce the heat to low then start adding the cheese, a little at a time, while stirring constantly in a figure of eight pattern.

When you've added all of the cheese, stir in the pepper and the mustard, and continue to stir for 1 minute.

Pour the cheese mixture into the fondue pot that is set over the burner and serve immediately.

Dunk in with crusty bread on skewers, or try corn chips, carrot batons and celery chunks.

Serves 4

INSALATA CAPRESE ON STICKS

This is a famous and simple Italian salad from the island of Capri. Like a lot of Italian dishes, simple works best, but you do need to use the best ingredients you can get your hands on.

4 balls of buffalo mozzarella (the number you need
    really depends on the size of the balls)
16 basil leaves
16 ripe cherry or plum tomatoes
3 tablespoons extra virgin olive oil

1 teaspoon fine sea salt
¼ teaspoon freshly ground black pepper
1 teaspoon oregano leaves, chopped
16 skewers

Cut the mozzarella into quarters (once again this depends on the size of the balls). On each skewer, thread a piece of mozzarella, a basil leaf and a tomato. Lay the skewers on a serving plate, drizzle them with the olive oil, and season with the sea salt, black pepper and oregano.

Makes 16

DAGWOOD (CORN) DOGS

Dagwood dogs—also known as corn dogs and pluto pups— always seem to show up at carnivals. They really have got a cult following in the United States, where they even celebrate National Corndog Day—which from what I gather consists of watching basketball, eating corndogs and drinking beer. Sounds like a pretty good way to spend the day to me. Dagwoods are generally large hotdogs, but I've gone for the mini version with this recipe.

20 cocktail frankfurts (hot dogs)
1 litre (36fl oz) vegetable oil
20 small skewers, forks or toothpicks

BATTER
1¼ cups plain (all-purpose) flour
¾ cup cornmeal (polenta)
3 tablespoons caster (superfine) sugar
1 teaspoon baking powder
2 eggs
¾ cup milk

For the batter, in a bowl whisk together the plain flour, cornmeal, caster sugar, baking powder, eggs and milk until the mixture is lump free. If it looks too thick, add a little water.

In a large saucepan or wok heat the oil: the oil is the right temperature when a little bit of batter into the oil rises to the top instantly.

Pat dry the frankfurts with a paper towel, insert the skewer into one end and place them in the batter while holding the stick, if the batter doesn't stick to the frankfurts, roll them in flour before battering. Cook in batches in the hot oil for around 5 minutes.

Serve with tomato sauce (ketchup) and, my personal favourite, corn relish.

Makes 20

TIP
Be very careful when deep-frying at
home: always use a bigger saucepan
or wok than you think you need to
avoid a boil-over.

DEVILS ON HORSEBACK

There is no way I was going to leave these bad boys out of any book I'm doing about food on sticks. These little devils were the first ever task I was given in a commercial kitchen, in my very first job. I remember it so vividly, mainly because I made them for two whole days straight—why they didn't buy pitted prunes still puzzles me to this day. I also remember being puzzled by the combination, until I eventually got around to trying one and discovering I quite liked it.

10 rashers streaky bacon
20 pitted soft, dried prunes

20 toothpicks

Cut the bacon strips in half across the middle. Lay the bacon strip flat, and tightly wrap the prune. Pierce through the bacon and the prune with a toothpick to hold it together.

Preheat your oven or grill to high. Place the wrapped prunes on a lightly oiled baking tray and cook them until the bacon is slightly crispy (around 10 minutes).

Makes 20

TIP
Traditionally the prune is stuffed with a little mango chutney, but I like to soak the prunes in some brandy for 15 minutes before I wrap them.

HAM AND PINEAPPLE KEBABS

When I was a kid, one of my favourite things to eat was ham steak and pineapple. We used to eat it as a big slab of ham topped with a tinned pineapple ring and a maraschino cherry on top. These skewers are a little more sophisticated, but offer a great trip down memory lane.

600g (1lb 5oz) good-quality ham cut into
    2½cm (1in) cubes
1 pineapple, peeled, cored and cut into cubes
8 maraschino cherries
vegetable oil, for the grill or pan
8 skewers

MARINADE
2 tablespoons honey
30ml (1fl oz) pineapple juice
1 tablespoon Dijon mustard

For the marinade, in a bowl, mix together the honey, pineapple juice and mustard. Add the ham, and mix through to coat the ham in the honey mixture.

Thread three pieces of ham and two pieces of pineapple onto each skewer. Top off with a cherry on the end of each skewer.

Cook on a preheated flat grill or frying pan with a little oil on medium–high heat, turning occasionally for 5 minutes.

Serve two skewers per person, with chips and a basic iceberg lettuce and tomato salad.

Serves 4

TIP
Tinned pineapple rings will work fine
in this recipe.

MILK CHOCOLATE FONDUE

MILK CHOCOLATE FONDUE

I guess I've never tried fondues before because I'm not a massive cheese fan—well that, and the fact that they're so darn kitsch. But if there's chocolate involved, then you can count me in! A fondue pot with a burner is needed here to keep the chocolate warm and liquid—then you're ready to go, and you've got yourself a wicked sharing dessert.

300ml (10fl oz) thickened cream

350g (12oz) good-quality milk chocolate, grated

1 pineapple, peeled, cored and cut into bite-sized chunks

3 bananas, cut into 2cm (¾in) thick slices

2 punnets (500g/17½oz) strawberries, hulled

1 punnet (250g/9oz) raspberries

1 packet marshmallows

long wooden skewers or fondue forks

Pour the cream into a saucepan and bring it slowly to the boil. Remove from the heat, and add the chocolate slowly, while stirring. When the chocolate has completely melted, pour the chocolate mixture into the fondue pot with the burner going gently underneath it.

Using sticks, dip the fruit and the marshmallows into the chocolate and then straight into your mouth. Have fun!

OYSTERS KILPATRICK

Oysters kilpatrick, or 'killas' as we called them back when I was an apprentice, were my introduction into the world of oysters. Having them kilpatrick was much easier to stomach for a 17-year-old than natural, and I still get the odd craving for them. Although it's not traditional, I like adding tomato sauce to the Worcestershire, as I feel it gives them a little more zing.

12 oysters

6 rashers streaky bacon

2 tablespoons Worcestershire sauce

1 tablespoon tomato sauce (ketchup)

300g (10oz) rock salt

12 toothpicks

chives, chopped (optional)

Remove the oysters from their shells.

Cut the bacon into 6cm (2½in) lengths. Wrap a piece of bacon tightly around each oyster and secure it with a toothpick.

In a small bowl, mix the two sauces together.

Place half the rock salt on a small oven tray and nestle the oyster shells in the rock salt. Place a bacon wrapped oyster in each shell, pour a little of the sauce mix into each and place the tray in a preheated, very hot oven—230°C (450°F)—or under the grill, and cook them until the bacon is coloured (about 3 to 4 minutes).

Pour the remaining rock salt onto a serving platter, and place the cooked oysters on top.

Makes 12

TIP

If you want to spice things up a little, add some tabasco to the sauce mix.

SURF AND TURF ON A STICK

A bistro classic—who hasn't at one time had a surf and turf or reef and beef down at the pub?

10 medium Canadian scallops
10 medium prawns (shrimp), shelled and cleaned,
   tails left on
500g (1lb) beef fillet, cleaned
1 medium red onion, peeled and cut into cubes
vegetable oil, for the grill or pan
10 skewers

MARINADE
1 small handful flat-leaf parsley, chopped
2 garlic cloves, finely chopped
50ml (2fl oz) olive oil
¼ teaspoon salt
¼ teaspoon freshly ground black pepper

For the marinade, in a bowl, mix together the parsley, garlic, oil, salt and pepper.

Cut the beef fillet into 20 pieces and then place them in the marinade bowl, and add the scallops and the prawns. Mix carefully to ensure everything is coated.

Thread two pieces of beef, one scallop and one prawn onto each skewer, placing a cube of onion between each.

Heat a little oil in a frying pan or on a flat grill and cook each skewer for around 1½ minutes each side.
Makes 10

TOFFEE APPLE

When I asked Adam (our head chef at Red Spice Road) to help out on the sweet sticks section, I should have known that we would be doing a toffee apple. He absolutely loves the things—they were even served at his engagement party!

10 Granny Smith apples

4 cups caster (superfine) sugar

1 cup hot water

2 teaspoons red food colouring

½ teaspoon cream of tartar

10 wooden chopsticks

Push the chopsticks into the apple core. Put the sugar and the water into a saucepan, and stir until the sugar has dissolved. Turn the heat up to high and add the red colouring and the cream of tartar, bring to the boil then turn down to a simmer and cook for around 15 minutes. To check if the toffee is ready, drop a teaspoon of toffee into ice-cold water, when you remove it from the water, you should be able crack the toffee easily.

Line a baking tray with non-stick baking paper. Dip the apples one at a time into the toffee, making sure you cover the apples entirely with the toffee. Remove the apples from the toffee, drain slightly and place them on the paper-lined tray. Allow to cool before serving, but do not refrigerate.

Serves 10

TIP
If the toffee starts to set while you're dunking your apples, return it to the heat to re-melt it.

SWEET STICKS

BANANAS WITH CHOCOLATE AND PEANUTS

These guys are pretty much a banana sundae on a stick. They're easy to prepare and cook on your barbecue and naturally go perfectly with vanilla ice cream

4 medium-sized bananas

2 tablespoons caster (superfine) sugar

1 tablespoon butter

150g (5oz) good-quality milk chocolate

100g (3½oz) good-quality white chocolate

3 tablespoons peanuts, chopped

12 skewers

Peel and slice the bananas into 1cm (½in) thick slices. Thread four pieces of banana onto each skewer. Sprinkle each skewer on both sides with the caster sugar.

In two stainless steel bowls, melt the milk and white chocolates separately over a water bath making sure that the bowls are not touching the water.

On a preheated flat grill or in a frying pan on high, melt the butter, then add the banana skewers and cook until they start to brown.

Remove them and place them on a serving plate, drizzle over the two chocolates and sprinkle with chopped nuts.

Makes 12

BANANAS WITH CHOCOLATE AND PEANUTS

CHOC, CHILLI AND MINT PARFAIT POPS

A parfait is basically an ice cream that you don't have to churn—it doesn't ice up because of its high sugar and fat content. The flavours in this parfait are a real treat for your senses—cold and refreshing, yet spicy. This recipe will make more than you need, as it's quite difficult to make it in small batches, so either make more pops or freeze it in small moulds.

175g (6oz) good-quality chocolate

3 egg whites

25g (1oz) caster (superfine) sugar, extra

375ml (13fl oz) thickened cream, whipped
    to soft peaks

75ml (2½fl oz) water

120g (4oz) caster (superfine) sugar

1 small red chilli, chopped

6 egg yolks

2 Peppermint Crisp chocolate bars (or other
    peppermint-flavoured chocolate), finely chopped

12 icy pole (popsicle) moulds

Melt the chocolate in a bowl over a water bath making sure that the bowl isn't touching the water.

In a mixer, beat the egg whites until soft peaks form, then add the extra 25g caster sugar and continue beating to form stiff peaks. Fold into the whipped cream and set aside.

In a small saucepan, add the water, 120g (4oz) caster sugar and the chilli. Bring to the boil, then simmer until the syrup gets to soft ball stage (see tip below), then strain and discard the chillies.

In a mixer, beat the yolks on high speed until they're thick and creamy. With the mixer running slowly, drizzle in the chilli sugar syrup and continue to mix for 5 minutes.

Add a little of the cream–egg white mixture to the chocolate, and mix together gently. Then add the cream mixture to this chocolate mixture and fold through gently. When everything is fully combined, pour in the egg yolk mix and the peppermint crisps, and once again fold in gently.

Pour the mixture into icy pole moulds and freeze overnight.

Makes 12

TIP

To check for soft ball consistency, drop a little of the sugar syrup into a bowl of cold water. A ball of sugar should form. If it doesn't, continue heating and try again.

HONEYED FIGS WITH WHIPPED LEMON GOAT'S CURD

Figs are such a luscious treat, but they are only in season for a really short time, so it's important to make these skewers while you have the chance.

9 figs, cut in half
2 tablespoons butter
3 tablespoons honey
1 pinch saffron
6 skewers

LEMON GOAT'S CURD
150g (5oz) goat's curd
30g (1oz) caster (superfine) sugar
1 tablespoon lemon juice
1 teaspoon finely grated lemon rind

Thread three fig halves onto each skewer.

Place the goat's curd, caster sugar and lemon juice in a food processor or a mixer, and blend until whipped and smooth. Place the curd in a bowl and mix the lemon rind through.

In a frying pan on low heat, combine the butter, honey and saffron. When the butter has melted, turn up the heat and stir so the ingredients are well combined.

Place the figs, open side down, in the frying pan and cook over a high heat for 1 minute. Turn the skewers over and cook for a further 30 seconds.

Place the fig skewers on a serving dish and pour some of the pan juices over them. Serve with the goat's curd.

Makes 6

MELON STICKS WITH VANILLA HONEY YOGHURT

These little guys are quite colourful and very healthy. You could also add other fruit, if you liked, such as pineapple or strawberries, but I like to use just melon. You'll need a melon baller to create the proper visual effect, although I guess cubes would work just fine too.

12 watermelon balls
12 rockmelon (cantaloupe) balls
12 honeydew melon balls
12 champagne melon balls
30ml (1fl oz) Malibu (coconut rum)
12 small skewers

VANILLA HONEY YOGHURT
2 vanilla beans
3 tablespoons honey
300ml (10fl oz) natural yoghurt

To make the yoghurt, start by cutting the vanilla beans down the middle and scraping out the vanilla seeds.

Heat the honey in a small saucepan, add the vanilla seeds and remove from the heat. Allow to cool to around room temperature. In a bowl, mix together the yoghurt and the vanilla honey mixture.

Put the melon balls into a bowl with the Malibu, give it a mix, and allow it to marinate for 10 minutes.

Thread a ball of each melon onto the skewers.

Spoon a little of the yoghurt mixture into a large shot glass and place a melon skewer in each glass.

Makes 12

MEXICAN PINEAPPLE AND ORANGE ICE POPS

Adam, my head chef, introduced me to ice pops a while ago. Ice pops are generally made with fresh fruit and usually contain chilli of some sort. Oh, and they taste great!

1 cup caster (superfine) sugar

2 cups water

1kg (2lb 4oz) pineapple, peeled cored and cut into small pieces

2 oranges, juiced

1 teaspoon cayenne pepper

15 icy pole (popsicle) moulds

In a saucepan, place the sugar and the water and stir to dissolve the sugar. Place the saucepan on the heat and bring to the boil. Turn turn down to simmer and continue to cook for around 5 minutes. We want the sugar to get to what we call soft ball stage, which is the stage before caramel. To test the sugar, drop a little in a glass of cold water and it should form a ball. If it doesn't, keep the syrup on the stove and try again.

Place the pineapple in a food processor and process into pulp. Remove the pineapple pulp from the processor into a bowl. Add the sugar syrup, orange juice and the cayenne pepper, and whisk to combine.

Pour into icy pole moulds and freeze overnight.

Depending on the size of your moulds, the mixture should make at least 15 icy poles.

Makes 15

> ### TIP
> Soft ball stage is roughly between 115°C and 120°C (about 250°F). If you have a candy thermometer you can also check that the mixture has reached the right temperature using the thermometer.

PEPPERED RUM-SOUSED PINEAPPLE

A bit of an unusual combo—but something a little different is always a good thing and the pepper really gives these skewers a great kick. Make sure your pineapple is ripe, because it makes the world of difference. They go really well with vanilla ice cream.

1 medium-sized ripe pineapple, skinned and cored
100g (3½oz) brown sugar
150ml (5fl oz) white rum

¼ teaspoon freshly ground black pepper
40g (1½oz) butter
6 skewers

Cut the pineapple into 4 cm (1½in) pieces.

In a bowl, mix the sugar and the rum until the sugar dissolves. Add the pineapple and allow it to sit for at least 15 minutes.

Thread four pieces of pineapple onto each skewer, and sprinkle with the pepper.

Melt the butter on a flat grill or in a frying pan and cook the pineapple for about 1½ minutes each side, taking care not to burn it.

Remove the skewers from the heat and serve immediately.

Makes 6

SAUCES

NUOC CHAM

A classic Vietnamese dipping sauce, nuoc cham also makes a great dressing. You can make it as hot or as sweet it suits you, just by adding more chilli or sugar.

2 garlic cloves
50ml (1¾fl oz) fish sauce
50ml (1¾fl oz) lime juice

50ml (1¾fl oz) rice vinegar
2 red bullet chillies, sliced
70g (2oz) caster (superfine) sugar

Mix all the ingredients in a bowl and stir until the sugar dissolves. Leave to stand for at least 30 minutes before using.

Makes around 200ml (7fl oz)

RED NAM JIM

This is probably the most widely used Thai dressing, as it is extremely versatile and pretty much goes with anything savoury. Feel free to alter the chilli, palm sugar, fish sauce, etc., to suit your taste.

4 large red chillies, seeded and chopped
1 small red chilli, chopped
3 coriander (cilantro) roots, chopped
2 garlic cloves, peeled and sliced

3 shallots (eschalots), peeled and thinly sliced
60g (2oz) palm sugar, grated
150ml (5fl oz) lime juice
80ml (2½fl oz) fish sauce

In a mortar and pestle, grind the chillies, coriander, garlic and shallots into a fine paste. Add the palm sugar, lime juice and fish sauce and mix well. Allow to sit for at least 10 minutes before using.

You can also use a blender or a food processor to make this dressing, although for some reason the mortar and pestle is always better. In a blender, just add all the ingredients together and blend.

Makes about 250ml (9fl oz)

TIP
If you can't get your hands on palm sugar, use brown sugar instead.

RED PEPPER AIOLI

Aioli is basically just a fancy mayonnaise. Like mayonnaise, it is very versatile as it goes just as well with fried food as it does raw vegetables. The red pepper definitely lifts this aioli way above the common mayonnaise.

2 egg yolks
1 tablespoon sherry vinegar
1 tablespoon lemon juice
1 tablespoon Dijon mustard

250ml (9fl oz) olive oil
50g (1¾oz) roasted red capsicums (bell peppers), peeled and finely chopped
1 pinch salt

To make the aioli, put the egg yolks, vinegar, lemon juice and Dijon mustard in a food processor and start blending. While the food processor is running, slowly drizzle in the olive oil and then add the red peppers, a pinch of salt and blend for a further 20 seconds.

Place the aioli in a bowl, cover and refrigerate for later use.

Makes around 350ml (12fl oz)

RIATA

Riata has its roots in Indian cuisine, and anybody who has sampled a hot Indian curry can certainly understand why. It's a fantastic and tasty cooling sauce that goes beautifully with anything spicy.

250ml (9fl oz) natural yoghurt
1 garlic clove, peeled and finely chopped
4 tablespoons cucumber, grated

3 tablespoons mint, chopped
¼ teaspoon salt

Place the cucumber in a tea towel and wring or press out the juice. Discard the juice. Place the cucumber in a mixing bowl, add the remaining ingredients and mix thoroughly. Cover and refrigerate for later use
Makes 300ml (10fl oz)

ROMESCO SAUCE

Romesco sauce hales from Catalonia in Spain. It has a great depth of flavour and is extremely versatile. Romesco probably teams up best with fish and seafood, but I think it goes well with most things—I even enjoy it on toast for breakfast.

1 whole garlic bulb
150ml (5fl oz) extra virgin olive oil
1 large ripe roma tomato
8 roasted almonds
8 roasted hazelnuts

1 thick slice of stale bread, crusts removed and
    turned into soft breadcrumbs
2 roasted red capsicums (bell peppers), skinned
1 small red chilli, finely chopped
50ml (1¾fl oz) sherry or red wine vinegar
½ teaspoon sea salt

Rub a little of the oil on the garlic bulb and place it on a baking tray. Repeat the process with the tomato. Place the tray in a hot oven preheated to 220°C (420°F) and roast them for 20 minutes. The garlic cloves should be soft and the tomato skin should be easy to remove. Take each clove individually and squeeze the garlic out.

Put the cooked garlic, tomato and the rest of the ingredients into a food processor and blend to a smooth paste.

Makes about 400g (14oz)

SWEET CHILLI SAUCE

I know what you're thinking: I can just buy this in a bottle at the supermarket. Well, this version is way superior to any version you can buy. It's worth making a reasonable amount of this sauce as it keeps really well in the refrigerator and it has so many uses.

15 large red chillies, seeded and chopped
3 garlic cloves, peeled and chopped
3 cups caster (superfine) sugar

1½ cups water
1½ cups rice vinegar
1 tablespoon salt

In a food processor, blend the chillies and the garlic into a paste.

Combine the sugar, water and vinegar in a saucepan, preferably with a heavy base. Bring to the boil, then add the chilli–garlic mix and the salt, and simmer for 10 minutes.

Store in an airtight container in the refrigerator.

Makes about 750ml (26fl oz)

SALSA VERDE

Once again, this is such a versatile sauce, it goes well with most meat and fish. It is really quite simple to make, and I love the beautiful vibrant green colour.

2 cups flat-leaf parsley leaves

1 cup basil leaves

2 spring onions (scallions), chopped

75g (2oz) small gherkins (cornichons)

75g (2oz) small capers

6 anchovy fillets

2 garlic cloves, peeled and finely chopped

4 tablespoons red wine vinegar

2 tablespoons lemon juice

100ml (3½fl oz) extra virgin olive oil

½ teaspoon sea salt

¼ teaspoon freshly ground black pepper

Place all the ingredients in a food processor. Process until well combined.

Makes about 400g (14oz)

TIP

It's always best to make salsa verde fresh, as the acid in the lemon juice and the vinegar will cause discoloration fairly quickly.

TZATZIKI

This version of tzatziki is so tasty when made fresh. It really is no fuss at all to make and a great way to impress your friends.

3 small Lebanese cucumbers, peeled, deseeded
and grated
2 garlic cloves, peeled and minced
1 handful mint leaves, chopped
1 small handful dill, chopped

2 tablespoons extra virgin olive oil
2 tablespoons lemon juice
250g (9oz) good-quality thick natural yoghurt
salt and pepper to taste

Squeeze the excess water out of the cucumber. Place the cucumber in a bowl. Add all the other ingredients, and mix thoroughly.

Store in the refrigerator until needed.

Makes about 400g (14oz)

GLOSSARY

Cardamom Used in Indian curries, as well as desserts. Comes in green and black varieties, as well as in pod or powder form.

Cayenne pepper Basically ground-up, dried chilli peppers.

Chillies We use a wide variety of chillies at Red Spice Road. Long red and green ones, as well as the smaller chillies, known as bullet or bird's eye, which are also red and green. As a rule of thumb, the smaller chillies are hotter, although it pays to check, because the larger ones can surprise you. Chilli also comes in flake and powder varieties as well.

Cornmeal Also known as polenta. A coarse flour ground from dried maize.

Crispy fried shallots can be bought in Asian supermarkets and are found increasingly in local supermarkets. They add a textural crunch as well as a nutty flavor to salads or stir-fries. *See also* shallots.

Cumin Used in many spice mixes and curry pastes. The seeds are brownish and small, and have a slightly aniseed flavour.

Dashi Comes in a number of different forms, the most popular being ground-up bonito granules. I think it's best described as tasty fish salt.

Fish sauce Used extensively in most Southeast Asian dishes, it's made from fermented fish, mostly anchovies. It's basically a salt, and it's extremely pungent. Never accidently spill it on your hair and then catch public transport home—trust me on this.

Galangal From the same family as ginger it's a bit spicier and stronger flavored as well as being more fibrous than ginger. It's used in most curry pastes.

Garam masala A spice powder commonly used in Indian cuisine. It's quite pungent in flavour and comes in various forms. Peppercorns, cloves, mace, cumin, cardamom, nutmeg, star anise and coriander seeds form the basis of garam masala.

Haloumi A semi-hard, unripened cheese made from a mixture of goat and sheep milk, although cow's milk can sometimes also be used.

Hoisin A popular Chinese sauce that contains a number of ingredients, including soybeans, sugar, garlic and a number of starches, such as sweet potato, rice and wheat. It can be used as a dipping sauce or as a flavouring.

Jamón The Spanish word for ham. It's the Spanish version of Italian prosciutto.

Kaffir lime leaf Glossy green leaves that generally come in pairs. They have a great citrus flavour and are essential in Southeast Asian cuisine. You can buy them fresh, frozen or dried—fresh is preferable, dried being what you should leave on the shelf. If the leaves are to be eaten, instead of just used as a flavouring and then removed, make sure they are sliced very finely. You can also use the rind of the kaffir lime fruit, which looks like a lumpy lime.

Lemongrass A beautifully flavoured long fibrous stalk. It's used extensively throughout Southeast Asia. You really can use only the paler bottom part. Great in soups, salads, desserts and curries, and even used as skewers.

Mirin Used in a lot of Japanese cooking, mirin is best described as a sweet rice wine. It comes in a few varieties that differ in sugar and salt content.

Shallots Basically small onions, they are also known as eschalots. Don't confuse them with spring or green onions.

Shaoxing or Chinese rice wine Used in the famous Chinese masterstock and a lot of other Chinese sauces and dressings. It has an earthy flavour.

Shiso Also called purple perilla, it has a strong original flavour and is used in salads as well as stir-fries.

Shrimp paste Used so much in Thai cooking, it is extremely pungent. Generally, it's first roasted by wrapping it in a banana leaf or aluminum foil and roasting it in the oven. It's used in curries and dressings. In Thailand it's called gapi, and in Malaysia, belacan.

Sichwan pepper This isn't actually a pepper, but rather the berry of a Chinese prickly ash tree. It has a tingling, numbing effect on your tongue.

Spring onions (scallions) These onions have a nice mellow onion flavour that is great in salads and stir-fries.

Tamarind Tamarind is actually a fruit. It is usually bought in a compressed block. It's used as a souring agent, like lime juice.

Tikka paste Extremely common Indian spice paste that you'll find on your local supermarket shelf.

Saffron threads The dried stamens from the saffron crocus plant, saffron is the world's most expensive spice—by weight it's actually more expensive than gold.

Sumac A red fruit that grows on small shrubs. The fruit forms dense clusters of what's called bobs. The sumac bobs are dried and ground to produce a tangy, lemony purple-red spice powder.

Turmeric Another relative of the ginger family, turmeric is a root that has a distinctive yellow colour and a strong, earthy flavour. It's available dried or fresh.

Zatar A spice commonly used in Middle Eastern cuisine. It's generally made up of oregano, thyme, savory, sumac and sesame seeds.

INDEX

Argentinean beef with chimichurri 10

Bananas with chocolate and peanuts 162
Barbecue pork and lychee sticks 13
Basil and garlic veg sticks 123
Bean shoot and sesame salad 76
beef
   Argentinean beef with chimichurri 10
   Bo la lot (beef wrapped in betel leaf) 16
   Haitian voodoo sticks (spicy beef kebabs) 20
   Lemongrass and sesame beef skewers 28
   Surf and turf on a stick 157
   Wagyu and rice meetballs with a quick red curry 48
Bo la lot (beef wrapped in betel leaf) 16
Burmese pork skewers 19

Cheese and beer fondue 142
Chicken liver, sage and beetroot skewers 91
Chicken sekuwa 86
Chicken tikka with cucumber salad and riata 88
Chicken yakitori 94
Chilled sesame yellowfin tuna with dashi mayo 57
Choc, chilli and mint parfait pops 167
Corn and green onion fritters 124

Dagwood (corn) dogs 145
Devils on horseback 146

Fiery prawn (shrimp) skewers 62
Five spice quail with Vietnamese slaw 111
fondue
   Cheese and beer fondue 142
   Milk chocolate fondue 153
fruit
   Bananas with chocolate and peanuts 162
   Barbecue pork and lychee sticks 13
   Devils on horseback 146
   Ham and pineapple kebabs 148

Honeyed figs with whipped lemon goat's curd 168
Melon sticks with vanilla honey yoghurt 171
Mexican pineapple and orange ice pops 172
Peppered rum-soused pineapple 173
Pineapple satay sauce 31
Pomegranate goat skewers 39
Toffee apple 158
Watermelon, feta and olive 138

Garlic and chilli prawns (shrimp) with lime aioli 64
Grilled Issan chicken 96

Haitian voodoo sticks (spicy beef kebabs) 20
Haloumi and Mediterranean vegetable kebabs 128
Ham and pineapple kebabs 148
Hiramasa Kingfish with soy, honey and ginger 67
Hoisin and ginger duck skewers 99
Honeyed figs with whipped lemon goat's curd 168

Indian-inspired turkey skewers 100
Insalata caprese on sticks 143
Issan sausages 23

Jamón-wrapped prawns (shrimp) 70
Jerk vegetable sticks 129
Joojeh kabab (Persian lemon and saffron chicken kebabs) 103

Lemon and oregano lamb skewers 24
Lemongrass and sesame beef skewers 28

Malaysian chicken satay 105
Melon sticks with vanilla honey yoghurt 171
Mexican pineapple and orange ice pops 172
Milk chocolate fondue 153
Minced pork on lemongrass sticks 29
Mushroom, eggplant (aubergine) and olive skewers 137

Nonya pork satay with pineapple satay sauce 30
Nuoc cham 176

Oysters kilpatrick 154

Patatas bravas 120
Peppered rum-soused pineapple 173
Peppered venison, beetroot and caramelised
    shallot pintxos 35
Pinchos moruno (Spanish-style skewers) 36
Pine nut salad 81
Pineapple satay sauce 31
Pomegranate goat skewers 39
Pork belly with chilli caramel 42
Portuguese-style chicken skewers 109
poultry
    Chicken liver, sage and beetroot skewers 91
    Chicken sekuwa 86
    Chicken tikka with cucumber salad and riata 88
    Chicken yakitori 94
    Five spice quail with Vietnamese slaw 111
    Grilled Issan chicken 96
    Hoisin and ginger duck skewers 99
    Indian-inspired turkey skewers 100
    Joojeh kabab (Persian lemon and saffron chicken
        kebabs) 103
    Malaysian chicken satay 105
    Portuguese-style chicken skewers 109
    Shish Taouk (Lebanese chicken skewers) 110
    Sumatran minced duck satay 115
    Thai grilled chicken satay 116
Prawn (shrimp) and chorizo skewers 58
Prawn (shrimp) wrapped sugar cane 71
Pureed parsnip 81

Red nam jim 178
Red pepper aioli 179
Riata 180
Romesco sauce 182
Rosemary potato skewers with melted tallegio 131

Salmon, potato, lemon and rosemary sticks 72
Salsa verde 184
Sate babi manis 44
seafood
    Chilled sesame yellowfin tuna with dashi mayo 57
    Fiery prawn (shrimp) skewers 62
    Garlic and chilli prawns (shrimp) with lime aioli 64
    Hiramasa kingfish with soy, honey and ginger 67
    Jamón-wrapped prawns (shrimp) 70
    Oysters kilpatrick 154
    Prawn (shrimp) and chorizo skewers 58
    Prawn (shrimp) wrapped sugar cane 71
    Salmon, potato, lemon and rosemary sticks 72
    Soy and five spice rainbow trout sticks with a bean
        shoot and sesame salad 75
    Soy and lemongrass salmon 79
    Soy, ginger and sesame calamari skewers 54
    Surf and turf on a stick 157
    The ultimate scallop brochette with pureed parsnip
        and pine nut salad 80
Shish Taouk (Lebanese chicken skewers) 110
Soy and five spice rainbow trout sticks with a bean
    shoot and sesame salad 75
Soy and lemongrass salmon 79
Soy, ginger and sesame calamari skewers 54
Spicy peanut sauce 106
Sumac and zatar lamb skewers 47
Sumatran minced duck satay 115
Surf and turf on a stick 157
Sweet chilli sauce 183
Sweet potato, asparagus and bocconcini sticks 132
sweets
    Bananas with chocolate and peanuts 162
    Choc, chilli and mint parfait pops 167
    Honeyed figs with whipped lemon goat's curd 168
    Melon sticks with vanilla honey yoghurt 171
    Mexican pineapple and orange ice pops 172
    Milk chocolate fondue 153
    Peppered rum-soused pineapple 173
    Toffee apple 158

Thai grilled chicken satay 116

The ultimate scallop brochette with pureed parsnip
   and pine nut salad 80

Toffee apple 158

Tofu, shiitake mushroom, wasabi and green onion
   sticks 136

Tomato achar 87

Tomato kebabs 104

Tzatziki 185

Vegetable

   Basil and garlic veg sticks 123

   Bean shoot and sesame salad 76

   Chicken liver, sage and beetroot skewers 91

   Chicken tikka with cucumber salad and riata 88

   Corn and green onion fritters 124

   Five spice quail with Vietnamese slaw 111

   Haloumi and Mediterranean vegetable kebabs 128

   Insalata caprese on sticks 143

   Jerk vegetable sticks 129

   Mushroom, eggplant (aubergine) and olive

   skewers 137

Patatas bravas 120

Peppered venison, beetroot and caramelised
   shallot pintxos 35

Pine nut salad 80

Pureed parsnip 80

Rosemary potato skewers with melted tallegio 131

Salmon, potato, lemon and rosemary sticks 72

Soy and lemongrass salmon 79

Sweet potato, asparagus and bocconcini sticks 132

Tofu, shiitake mushroom, wasabi and green onion
   sticks 136

Tomato achar 87

Tomato kebabs 104

Wagyu and rice meetballs with a quick red curry 48

Watermelon, feta and olive 138

Wagyu and rice meatballs with a quick red curry 48

Watermelon, feta and olive 138

Xinjiang lamb kebab 51

ACKNOWLEDGEMENTS

Heaps of thanks to all my kitchen team, especially Adam, Marty, Justin, Dewan, Emma, Jenny and Khan. Without their support I would not have been able to start, let alone complete, this book. Thanks also to our amazing office staff, Rachel, Emma and Steph.

A very special thanks to my partner at Red Spice Road, Gavin Van Staden, who is forever helping me in one way or another. I couldn't imagine our restaurant without you mate.

Without the support I get from the owner of Red Spice Road, Andrew Cameron, I wouldn't be able to work on projects such as this book. Thanks Andrew: I appreciate you very much.

Thanks to Fiona Schultz and all the staff at New Holland Publishers for showing so much faith in me, as well as being patient regarding deadlines. Also to Linda Williams and her partner, Peter Turner, for finding Red Spice Road and falling in love with us.

To all my mates who are extremely important to me and keep me sane: Shaun Moorhouse, Varun Sharma (pass monkey), Faik Kenger, Carl Kooprogge, James Robertson, Bruce Sinclair, Michael Hartley, Craig Cavanaugh and David Lloyd—thanks boys.

To all my former employers, Peter and Maria Neville who are great friends; Jose and Sandra DeOliveiara; Damien Trytell and especially Cath Claringbold—thank you.

Special thanks to Adam Trengove for not only being a fantastic chef but also the best friend anybody could hope for. Also thank you so much for contributing some recipes for the book.

And to my beautiful wife, Alicia, the biggest thanks of all. You're a fantastic person Alicia and I love you very much.

First published in 2012 by
New Holland Publishers Pty Ltd
London • Sydney • Cape Town • Auckland

Garfield House 86–88 Edgware Road London W2 2EA United Kingdom
1/66 Gibbes Street Chatswood NSW 2067 Australia
218 Lake Road Northcote Auckland New Zealand
Wembley Square First Floor Solan Road Gardens Cape Town 8001 South Africa

www.newhollandpublishers.com
www.newholland.com.au

A record of this book is held at the National Library of Australia.

ISBN 9781742572376

Publisher: Linda Williams
Publishing director: Lliane Clarke
Project editor: Jodi De Vantier
Designer: Kimberley Pearce
Photographs: Graeme Gillies
Food stylist: Fiona Riggs
Production director: Olga Dementiev
Printer: Toppan Leefung Printing Ltd (China)

10 9 8 7 6 5 4 3 2 1

Keep up with New Holland Publishers on Facebook and Twitter.
www.facebook.com/NewHollandPublishers

UK £16.99
US $19.99